MOREHOUSE FARM

Merino Knits

MOREHOUSE FARM
Merino Knits

More than 40 Farm-Fresh Designs

Margrit Lohrer

Photography by Clara Aich

POTTER
CRAFT

NEW YORK

Published in the United States by Potter Craft,
an imprint of the Crown Publishing Group,
a division of Random House, Inc., New York.
www.crownpublishing.com
www.clarksonpotter.com

POTTER CRAFT and CLARKSON N. POTTER are
trademarks, and POTTER and colophon are
registered trademarks of Random House, Inc.

Library of Congress Cataloging-in-Publication
Data is available

ISBN 1-4000-9744-4

Printed in China

Design by Claire Vaccaro

Photography by Clara Aich

10 9 8 7 6 5 4 3 2 1

First Edition

TO MY TWO FAVORITE PEOPLE:

my mother, Sophie Lohrer

and my husband, Albrecht Pichler

AND TO MY FAVORITE ANIMAL:

Merino sheep

ALSO—MANY, MANY THANKS TO:

Marie Aimi	Henry Potter
Jeff and Debbie Traver	Kim Robbins
MarieElena Potter	MaryPat Davies
Molly Potter	Erin Sepe
Isabella Potter	Theresa Bentz

CONTENTS

INTRODUCTION

Morehouse Farm began with a voodoo chicken.

In the late 1970s, my husband Albrecht and I were both living and working in New York City, I as a graphic designer and he as an architect. One day, on my way to work, I found a white chicken running across Riverside Drive, a busy thoroughfare on Manhattan's Upper West Side. The road runs parallel to a park where the sight of dead chickens and goats—decked out in carnations and other voodoo rites paraphernalia—was not uncommon. This white chicken must have escaped! I caught it and took it to work, figuring I would take it to our upstate farm the following weekend. Imagine the sight of me: riding up an elevator in an office building with a briefcase under one arm and a live chicken under the other!

Albrecht and I had purchased the farm in Milan, New York, in 1977 as a weekend getaway. We promised each other that we would stop smoking the minute the farm was ours—and we've both kept our promise. We also thought that perhaps we might retire to the farm someday and raise animals. And that weekend we began our livestock collection with the rescued chicken to the farm. We hammered together a chicken coop in the barn and imagined the fresh eggs we would eat for breakfast. We bought a brown hen and black hen from a neighboring farm to keep this lonely voodoo survivor company. The two hens went to work the very next day and each laid an egg. Not so

Above: The voodoo chicken gets a pedicure.

Opposite: Empty pastures waiting for the arrival of the sheep.

with the voodoo chicken. We waited several weeks and made jokes about the New York City chicken not being a true country hen, until one morning we heard the reason for the chicken's reluctance to lay eggs: it was crowing at four o'clock in the morning. The chicken was a rooster and not an egg-laying hen.

After this inauspicious start, we decided that it was time to farm in earnest—not chickens, but sheep. My husband and I love all animals, but are particularly fond of sheep. We like the idea of turning grass into knitting wool. We named our farm Morehouse Farm after the former owners of the surrounding land.

WHY MERINO SHEEP

In researching the subject of sheep, we read over and over that Merinos grow the finest, most valuable wool and are the best wool-producing animals. Merino is one of the oldest breeds of sheep. Where they

A handsome pair of Merino rams.

originally came from no one knows for sure: some say the agriculturally skilled Moors in Spain were responsible for breeding the animals; others give credit to the Romans.

In the Middle Ages, Spain's wealth was based on the fine wool grown by their Merino sheep (I once read that Columbus's trip to this country was financed with merino wool). It was a capital offense to sell, export, or smuggle Merino sheep out of Spain. Owned by rulers and noblemen, the sheep were herded over great distances from the north of Spain to winter quarters in the south and back up north for the summer. These long treks may be the reason for the Merino sheep's highly developed flocking instinct (which is much stronger than in any other breed of sheep), because stragglers simply didn't survive the marches through Spain.

The Spanish monopoly on Merinos ended when Napoleon Bonaparte invaded Spain in the early 1800s. Soon, flocks of Merino sheep were dispersed all over the world. Shiploads of sheep crossed the ocean where American buyers were eagerly awaiting them. In 1815 Merino rams sold for a thousand dollars only to be resold for a buck a piece as mutton a dozen years later when the Merino craze subsided. And in the mid-1980s, with fine-wool pieces at an all-time high, an Australian Merino was auctioned off for half a million dollars. The roller coaster popularity of Merino sheep will no doubt continue, but there's no denying that when it comes to wool, Merinos are leaders of the flock and are the source of the legendary golden fleece.

MODERN-DAY ARGONAUTS

So we decided to raise Merino sheep because we wanted Morehouse Farm to become a mecca for knitters. Our next step was to find Merino sheep. That turned out to be easier said than done in the early 1980s. Merino sheep had all but disappeared, especially here in the Eastern United States. They had lost favor with most American sheep farmers and were generally not well thought of; "greasy, wrinkly, and dirty" were the adjectives most often used by livestock experts when describing Merino sheep. But we were determined to resurrect the reputation of

Pumpkin, the first ram lamb born at Morehouse.

Trimming hooves.

this once-popular animal. In 1983 we bought our first Merino sheep. We purchased the winning flock—three ewes and one ram—at the Harrisburg Livestock Show in Pennsylvania from a breeder from Ohio. Renting a moving van, we hauled them to our farm in upstate New York. That evening, while unloading the sheep, the ram jumped out of the truck and headed straight for one of the ewes and mated her right then and there. Five months later our first ram lamb was born. We named him Pumpkin.

We put together an ambitious five-year plan for the future of our farm. This plan included the sale of breeding stock, especially rams. But first we had to create demand for a breed of sheep that not many farmers were eager to purchase and raise.

Our dream to grow the finest wool came to fruition in an unexpected way—with help from the global economy. While visiting an international sheep congress held in Canada, Albrecht and I came across the Australian sheep delegation's exhibit of a fleece from a superfine Merino sheep. It was the most incredibly beautiful wool we had ever seen, white as snow and light as a cloud. This was it! This was the type of wool we wanted to grow. In Australia, the Merino is the most popular breed of sheep and its wool is classified as strong, medium, fine, superfine, and even ultrafine. The next day I called the Australian Livestock Association and inquired about importing some of those incredible animals.

That plan turned out to be a lot more complicated than we had anticipated. The Australians were equally protective of their fine-wool Merino sheep as the Spaniards were several hundred years earlier. Only five hundred rams were to be sold annually to the outside world (that was in 1984; the rules have changed since). And to complicate matters, these precious few animals were to be sold off at a government-sponsored auction. Finally, a year later, two rams were on their way to our New York farm (via Hawaii after several months quarantine). They arrived just as the price for fine wool went through the roof. We advertised the sale of semen from our two Aussie rams, and the demand was so great that within three years we surpassed the financial goals of our five-year plan. The price for fine-wool Merino rams jumped up and our breeding stock program was on a roll.

For the first few years we farmed on weekends and pursued our professional careers in New York City during the week. Every weekend I would rub my woolen mittens in the sheep's wool so that I could get a whiff of farm and sheep while in the office. In 1990, I said goodbye to city life and embarked on my new career as sheep farmer.

SPINNING A GOOD YARN

To showcase our flock's soft merino wool, we spin it into different weights of yarn, from bulky to lace, in over sixty colors. The process of turning our merino wool into yarn is an odyssey. Once a year, a crew of professional shearers comes to the farm to shear the flock. Skilled professionals are needed to shear Merino sheep because hidden under a year's growth of wool are lots of skinfolds. It takes two to three days for the entire flock to be shorn. Then the shorn wool, called fleece, is sorted by color and by quality. The cleaner parts are separated from the dirtier pieces and all are bagged in large polypropylene bags. A mechanical wool baler compresses the wool further in the bags until they are packed solid and each bale will weigh several hundred pounds.

Then we truck the wool bales to a scouring plant ("scouring" is the technical word for washing wool). In our case that means hauling wool halfway across the country, from New York to the closest scouring plant in Texas—that's right, Texas! There the wool is washed in large vats with hot water and soap. One of the by-products of this washing process is lanolin. Lanolin is the natural grease in sheep wool (it coats the wool to protect it from the elements). And lanolin, of course, is used as a base in cosmetics and lotions.

After washing, the wool is fluff dried and pressed back into bales again. Next stop: the spinning mill in New England. The fluffy wool is carded to untangle the tufts and straighten the fibers. The carding machine consists of large rotating rollers with hundreds of tiny spikes protruding. From the carding machine the wool (called batting at this stage) is separated into thin strips called pencil roving and wound onto spools. The spools are then set up on the spinning frame, where a

Hugging a ram, winter 1992.

My mother, Sophie, on the four-wheeler.

THE LONELY RAM

Albrecht winding yarn for my knitting projects at one of the rest stops en route to Wyoming.

In 1992, Albrecht and I were trucking sheep across the country, delivering rams to Utah, Nevada, and Wyoming. We were on the way to our final destination, a small town called Ten Sleep, Wyoming, with a single ram in the trailer. Over the mountainous roads to Ten Sleep, the brakes on our truck were getting soft and we were getting worried and tired. We decided to pull into one of those roadside campsites with our livestock trailer, which thankfully has living quarters for people as well. No sooner had we parked our rig, than the ram in the back started to bah. Merino sheep are gregarious creatures; nothing upsets them more than being alone. To calm him down, we let him hang around the trailer while we ate our dinner. When it was time to go to sleep, we put him back into the trailer . . . and his complaining started again. The neighboring campers got upset, too. We were too tired to go on; we needed a night's sleep and so did the neighbors. So what were we to do with the lonely ram in the back of the trailer calling for his buddies? We grabbed our blankets and headed for the trailer where we slept in the straw together with the ram. He was content with the arrangement, the neighbors quieted down, and Albrecht and I—well, we can say we bedded down with a ram.

machine unravels the pencil roving and twists it into yarn and winds the yarn back onto spools again. If the yarn is to be plied (for thicker yarn), the spools will be unraveled once more and another machine will twist several strands together. After a steam bath to set the twist, the knitting yarn is wound into skeins or balls.

For the first five years of our operation, we never considered dyeing our merino yarn. Our natural colors were colorful enough, and we never tired of knitting and weaving with them. That all changed, however, when we started attending the greenmarkets in New York City. Imagine displaying our yarn next to fruit and vegetable stands. Our natural colors seemed drab compared to bright red strawberries, golden apples, and fresh green vegetables. We had to compete—quite literally—with the tomatoes! So we started dyeing some of our merino yarn bright colors. And we have been doing it ever since.

Dyed yarn as colorful as fresh fruits and vegetables.

CONFESSIONS OF A LIFE-LONG KNITTER

It is no coincidence that my desire to farm found its inspiration in sheep and, eventually, producing knitting yarn. My mother taught me to knit when I was about four years old and I've been knitting ever since. I grew up in Switzerland where knitting was part of the school curriculum. I spent ten years learning to sew, knit, crochet, stitch, and darn. I still have my copy of the knitting book that I learned from— it's a small booklet, about eighty pages long. It contains only the basics; the rest we had to figure out ourselves. That book has been the foundation for my approach to knitting and designing. Make it up, design it yourself, figure it out—then cast on and start knitting!

It was also during my childhood that I came to appreciate the value of wool. My kindergarten teacher gave me the best gift I had ever received: three balls of green yarn from a sweater she was unraveling. This was a few years after World War II, and yarn was very scarce. Knitting was mainly possible by unraveling something old and worn, then reusing the yarn to knit something new. My dolls, including my stuffed giraffe, all sported green knits. To this day, I still very much value yarn, especially the fine wool from Merino sheep.

My approach to knitting is pretty simple: I want to knit, knit, and knit some more. My favorite projects are yards of scarves and acres of blankets. Stop-and-go projects bother me—stop and check, stop and read, stop and count—they don't give me time to think. Knitting is the time when I digest the day's events, my life's, and the world's. Life's meaning, for me, resides in the rhythm of knitting. And to come to grips with what's happening around us in this world of flashing images, quick talkers, and meaningless sound bites, you need hours of knitting. The blanket in this book (page 25) was by far my favorite project. It provided me with an entire week's worth of uninterrupted knitting!

Lots of knitting to be done here.

THE PATTERNS

For this book, I've designed patterns for sweaters, shawls, scarves, hats, mittens, as well as accessories for your home. None of the patterns are particularly challenging, but all will yield attractive and functional knitted items.

I've knit up the samples in this book with plenty of color variations to inspire you to knit on your own and to free you from thinking that you have to get a specific yarn or color because otherwise whatever you are knitting won't look right.

The patterns in this book are a starting point. Be creative and think of your own likes and dislikes. Knit what *you* want, the way *you* want it to look, feel, and wear. It's more satisfying to knit your own creation than to simply follow mine or other designers' patterns. The Molas Mitts and the Buggy Mitts are good examples of how you can personalize each one to make them uniquely yours.

Enjoy! The book, the patterns, and the snapshots of life at Morehouse Farm.

CHAPTER ONE

HOME

To personalize your surroundings, think about knitting for your home. Store-bought home accessories usually come in a limited color selection—that means whatever colors are in vogue at that moment (avocado or teal) and very little (or no) choice in the type of material.

My leather sofa needed a soft touch to make it a more inviting place to sit and read. Our burnt orange merino wool yarn was the perfect color and provided the softness I wanted for comfort. For the pillow, I added stripes of lilac to brighten and broaden the color scheme and to match my floor-length curtains. Where could I have purchased this custom look?

And sleeping under a bed-sized, hand-knit merino blanket is the absolute tops in treats. Knit one up as an incredibly fabulous gift for a pair of newlyweds; they'll live not only happily, but cozily ever after.

TUFTED CHAIR PAD AND CAT MAT

SIZE
About 16" x 16" (40.5cm x 40.5cm).

YARN
Worsted-weight wool yarn, about 450 to 500 yards (411.5 to 457m); small amounts of yarn in different colors for tufts. Use a yarn that felts well since the pillowcase will be felted slightly in washing machine.

The samples are knit with Morehouse Merino 3-Strand in Charcoal with Dusty Rose tufts for patio chair pad, in Emerald with tufts in miscellaneous colors for Buffy's cat mat, and in Black and Natural White with tufts in Fuchsia and Cardinal Red for chair pad; 3 skeins for each pillow.

NEEDLES
Size 4 or 5 (3.5 or 3.75mm): 24" (60cm) circular (or longer), or size to obtain gauge, and 1 extra needle, same size or slightly smaller, for three-needle bind-off.

GAUGE
20 stitches and 28 rows = 4 inches (10cm) in stockinette stitch pattern, before washing and felting. If you knit the pillow tightly, there will be very little shrinkage widthwise in the washing and felting process; however, the length will shrink between 15% and 20%, depending on the type of yarn you are using.

OTHER MATERIALS:
Polyester fiberfill or other washable stuffing, or 16" x 16" (40.5cm x 40.5cm) pillow form. For the chair pad use 2"- (5cm) thick foam rubber; strong cotton string to attach tufts to pillow; tapestry needle; stitch markers.

Opposite: I fell in love with this patio chair because of the shepherd, sheep, and peeling paint on the back-rest. To make the chair more comfortable, I added the pad, matching the tufts to the paint.

Colorful tufts add a touch of fun to these chair pads, and they prevent the stuffing from shifting around when you wash the pillows. Choose colors that match whatever suits your fancy: peeling paint on the patio furniture, or even the cat itself. I think Buffy (page 22) looks fantastic on emerald. Since the tufts and pillow are felted, future washings will not result in unwanted shrinkage.

FELTING

Before you begin these projects, knit a swatch using the yarn color(s) you plan to use. Cast on 30 stitches and knit 30 to 50 rows. Then measure the swatch, or better still, make a photocopy of it. That way you'll have an image of the original to measure against after felting the swatch. Felt the swatch in the washing machine using warm or hot water, depending on the type of yarns you are using, and how much felting you want. Hot water will felt fibers more drastically. Switching water temperatures from a hot-water wash to a cold-water rinse will produce more felting action than using a warm-water wash and rinse. Note the size of the original swatch before felting, and the washing procedure used, on an index card and pin the card to the felted swatch. Or, use the photocopy of the original and write down the washing procedure, then pin the swatch to the photocopy.

The cushion is knit as a tube and should fit (after felting) snugly around the pillow form. Cast on 160 stitches. Join stitches in a circle and knit in rounds until the pillow measures 19" (48.5cm).

Bind off as follows: with right side facing out, align both ends of the circular needle parallel to each other, with half the stitches at the front of the needle and the other half at the other end of the needle (let the plastic loop of the circular needle stick out at middle of round by bending it into a figure eight). Now bind off

both sides of pillow using three-needle bind-off as follows: with the extra needle, knit the first stitch on needle closest to you together with first stitch on needle in back, knit second stitch on needle closest to you together with second one on needle in back, then bind off in the usual manner by lifting first stitch over second one. Continue this way, knitting two stitches together as you bind off. Weave in yarn tails.

FINISHING

Felt the cushion following the washing procedure marked on your index card. Lay flat to dry. When the cushion is completely dry, insert pillow form or stuffing and sew the cast-on edges together to close.

TUFTS

Cut a piece of cardboard about ³/₄" (2cm) wide and about 5" (12.5cm) long. Make two slits on top then cut an 8" (20.5cm) piece of cotton string and insert into slits (see illustration at right). Wrap yarn loosely around cardboard and string 24 times. Slide wraps off cardboard and tie together with cotton string. Make between 5 and 9 tufts (in different colors for the Cat Mat or all in one color for the Chair Pad). Then put tufts through the washing machine on the knit or gentle cycle.

Here's another look at Buffy's emerald mat with multicolored tufts; to the left of it is my desk-chair pad. It sits on a gray desk chair at a gray desk in front of a gray computer—the black and white stripes and bright red and fuchsia tufts liven up an otherwise drab scene.

TUFTS TECHNIQUES

The washing action will tangle the wraps together and make them look more like tufts and less like loops—but don't cut the loops open. When tufts are dry, take both ends of the cotton string that's tied around each tuft and insert the ends through the stuffed pillow, spacing them about 1/2" (1.3cm) apart. For double-sided tufts, insert tufts on both sides of the pillow at the same location, then tie the two tufts together.

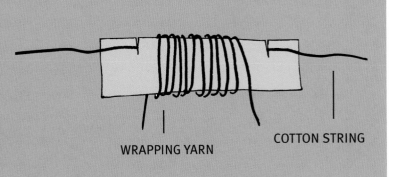

WRAPPING YARN   COTTON STRING

STRIPED BLANKET AND MATCHING PILLOWS

Approach this blanket project as you would plan a quilt: gather fabric colors—in this case yarn colors—that will work well together and look good in your home. You'll be creating a large surface, so keep the scope of the project in mind when choosing hues. You may want to combine different weights of yarns for a textured blanket.

Pillows are an easy way to update a room. If the colors are supposed to match those of the throw or the blanket, use them in a different sequence or narrow the stripes for a new effect.

Knit a swatch with all the yarns and colors you plan to use, then felt the swatch. If you don't like the way the felted swatch looks, change yarns or colors and make a second swatch, then felt it. Repeat this procedure until you are happy with the look and feel of the swatch. This is not the project to be casual about—you'll have spent a great deal of time knitting the blanket and you'll want the results to be worth all that time, effort, and material.

BLANKET

NOTE The blanket is knit in the round as a big, long tube. It is then washed, felted slightly, and laid flat to dry. To avoid wavy edges, don't cut the blanket open until it is completely dry. Rotate it several times during the drying process to prevent creases from forming. When completely dry, cut the blanket open between the first and last stitch of rounds.

Make a swatch using all the colors you plan to use for the blanket. Cast on 30 stitches and knit 30 to 50 rows. Then measure the swatch (or better yet, make a photocopy of it—that way you'll have an image of the original to measure against after felting the swatch). Felt the swatch in the washing machine using warm or hot water, depending on the type of yarns you are using and how much felting you want.

SIZE
Width: About 50" to 55" (127 to 140cm).
Length: 70" to 80" (178 to 203cm).

YARN
Worsted-weight wool yarn in four colors, about 3,600 yards (3,292m) total. 2,200 yards (2,012m) in main color, 450 yards (411.5m) each in 3 colors; plus about 60 yards (55m) of white or light color for border at beginning and end of blanket.

The sample is knit with Morehouse Merino 3-Strand in Smokey Pearl with stripes in Sunflower, Fuchsia, and Sienna; 15 skeins in main color, 3 skeins each in 3 colors, and small amount of white for border.

NEEDLES
Size 4 or 5 (3.5 or 3.75mm): 29" (73.5cm) circular, or longer.

OTHER MATERIALS
Tapestry needle.

GAUGE
20 stitches and 28 rows = 4 inches (10cm) in stockinette stitch pattern. If you knit the blanket tightly, there will be very little shrinkage widthwise in the washing and felting process; however, the length will shrink between 15% and 20%, depending on the type of yarn you are using.

Opposite: This blanket was one of my favorite knitting projects. It provided hours and hours of plain knitting, which allowed for hours and hours of uninterrupted thinking and dreaming. What bliss! The neutral brown-gray background and the bold, colorful stripes of this piece jazz up our barn hideaway.

Above: Tecumseh (or Cumsee for short), another Morehouse cat, watching our activities, or, more likely, eyeing the chickadees.

Opposite: Colorful swatches hanging from a tree, mimicking leaves.

Hot water will felt fibers more drastically. Switching water temperatures from a hot-water wash to a cold-water rinse will produce more felting action than using a warm-water wash and warm-water rinse. Note the size of the original swatch and the washing procedure used on an index card, and pin the card to the felted swatch. Or, use the photocopy, write down the washing procedure, and then pin the felted swatch to the photocopy for future reference.

Use your felted swatch to determine the number of stitches to cast on: 30 stitches divided by the width (in inches or centimeters) of your swatch = stitches or gauge per inch or centimeter. Now multiply this gauge (number of stitches) by the width (in inches or centimeters) of the blanket you want to knit. That will be the number of stitches to cast on for your blanket size.

With light color yarn for border, cast on between 250 and 280 stitches, or the number of stitches based on your swatch and blanket size.

> NOTE Cut yarn after each stripe, leaving a 3" to 4" tail . Tie the yarn tails together from beginning of new stripe and end of previous stripe to secure ends. Don't darn in ends, except the border color at cast-on and bind-off.

Join the cast-on stitches into circle, place marker between the first and last stitch to mark beginning of round. Knit 3 rounds. *Switch to color A (main color) and knit 24 rounds. Switch to color B and knit 16 rounds. With color A knit 24 rounds, then switch to color C and knit 16 rounds. With color A knit 24 rounds. Switch to color D and knit 16 rounds*.

Knit in stripe sequence from * to * until blanket measures 15% to 20% longer than desired length, depending on how much your swatch shrank. Finish blanket with 24 rounds in color A, followed by 3 rounds in light color for border, then bind off very loosely.

FINISHING

Felt the blanket following the washing procedure you've marked on your index card. While washing, rearrange the blanket several times in the washing machine to avoid bunching and an unevenly felted blanket. Lay the blanket flat to dry—don't cut it open yet—and

FELTING KNITS IN THE WASHING MACHINE

With the washing machine set for the knit cycle, add a little mild dishwashing liquid such as Palmolive to a warm-water wash and select a warm-water rinse. My moderate approach to felting may mean that you'll have to run the knitting through the washing machine again and again to get the result you want. My reasoning: you can always felt more, but you cannot correct what's been felted too much.

When felting large items such as a coat or a blanket, I stand by the machine with a cup of coffee and the newspaper and rearrange the contents of the machine every two minutes to avoid bunching and uneven felting.

I lay the item flat to dry on my bed. When it is completely dry—and only then—I may decide to felt the item some more and I'll repeat the procedure, shortening the duration of the wash cycle by a few minutes.

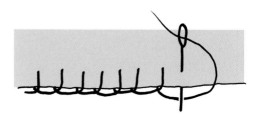

BLANKET STITCH

SIZE
15" x 20" (38cm x 51cm) or 16" x 16" (40.5cm x 40.5cm).

YARN
Worsted-weight wool yarn in two to three colors, about 450 yards (411.5m) total. Use a yarn that felts well because the pillowcase will be felted slightly in the washing machine. The samples are knit with Morehouse Merino 3-Strand in (from top down in photo opposite) Sienna with Lilac, Smokey Pearl with Natural White, and Fuchsia with Sienna; 2 skeins in main color, 1 skein in a contrasting color.

NEEDLES
Size 4 or 5 (3.5 or 3.75mm): 24" (61cm) circular (or longer), or size to obtain gauge, and 1 extra needle, same size or slightly smaller, for three-needle bind-off.

OTHER MATERIALS
Finished pillow form about 15" x 20" (38cm x 51cm) or 16" x 16" (40.5cm x 40.5cm), tapestry needle.
If you are using a pillow form with polyester fiberfill, the finished pillow will be machine washable; if you are using a down- or feather-filled form, dry clean the pillow.

GAUGE
20 stitches and 28 rows = 4 inches (10cm) in stockinette stitch pattern. The row gauge will be about 32 rows per 4 inches after felting.

rotate it several times during the drying process to prevent creases. When the blanket is completely dry, cut it open between the first and last stitches along the entire length of the blanket.

If you want the edges to have a more finished look, sew the blanket binding along the sides or around the entire blanket or finish the edges with a blanket stitch in a contrasting color (also see Baby Blanket on page 76).

MATCHING PILLOWS

Make a swatch with the yarn colors you are planning to use for the pillowcase following the same instructions for the felted blanket on page 25.

The pillow is knit as a tube and should fit snuggly (after felting) around pillow form. To make the 15" (38cm) pillow, cast on 150 stitches; to make the 16" (40.5cm) pillow, cast on 160 stitches. If your swatch shrank widthwise, adjust number of stitches accordingly. Follow the instructions for blanket on page 26 to determine your gauge and number of stitches.

Join the cast-on stitches into a circle, place marker between the first and last stitch to mark beginning of round. Knit in stripe pattern beginning with 6 to 10 rounds in main color, followed by 2 to 4 rounds in contrasting color. For the 20" (51cm) pillow length, you may want to start and end the pillow with a 4" (10cm) or 28 rounds wide stripe, then work the narrower stripe pattern (4 to 10 rounds each) for the middle 14" (35.5cm).

To complete the 16" x 16" (40.5cm x 40.5cm) size pillow, knit in stripe pattern until the pillow measures 19" (48.5cm) from the cast-on edge. To complete the 15" x 20" (38cm x 51cm) pillow, knit in pattern until piece measures 23" (58.5cm) in length. Bind off as follows: with right side facing out, place both ends of circular needle parallel to each other with half the stitches at one end of the needle, and the other half at the other end of the needle (let the plastic loop of the circular needle stick out at middle of round by bending it into a figure eight). Now bind off both sides of pillow using three-needle bind-off as follows: with the extra needle, knit the first stitch on needle closest to you together with the first stitch on needle in back, then knit the second stitch on needle closest to you together with the second stitch on needle in back, then bind off in the usual manner by lifting the first stitch on the extra needle over the second one. Continue this way, knitting two stitches together from front and back needle and binding off.

FINISHING

Felt the pillowcase following your washing procedure marked on the index card. Lay pillowcase flat to dry. When completely dry, insert the pillow form or stuffing and sew cast-on edges together to close the pillowcase.

A stack of my pillows—bolder and brighter is my motto for knitting these.

KNITKNOT THROW
AND WRAP

SIZE (after washing and blocking)
Width: About 54" (137cm).
Length: About 60" (152.5cm), not including
fringe.

YARN
Bulky-weight yarn, about 550 yards (503m)
and sport-weight yarn, about 700 yards
(640m).

The sample is knit with Morehouse Merino
Bulky in Sienna, 5 skeins; and Morehouse
Merino 2-Ply, 3 skeins.

NEEDLES
Size 15 (10mm): 29" (73.5cm) circular (or
longer). The throw is knit back and forth, but
you must have access to the stitches from
both ends of the needle because the working
yarn will be at the far end of the needle when
row 2 of pattern begins.

OTHER MATERIALS
Tapestry needle.

GAUGE
About 10 stitches = 4 inches (10cm) in pattern.
After washing and blocking, this pattern will
expand widthwise—not much lengthwise—
and the final gauge will be around
8 stitches = 4 inches (10cm).

*Opposite: The rust-colored throw and pillow make our
leather sofa a more comfortable and inviting place to sit
and read (or knit).*

The combination of yarns and the stitch pattern in this design make
the stitch loops of the bulky yarn look like they are knotted, rather
than knit together with thin yarn—that's why I've named this throw
and wrap "KnitKnot."

THROW

> NOTE This is a self-fringing throw. With every row knit with the bulky
> yarn, leave an 8" (20.5cm) yarn tail at beginning and end of row.

With sport-weight yarn, cast on 115 stitches. Knit one row then
switch to bulky yarn and start stitch pattern beginning with row 1.

STITCH PATTERN

ROW 1   (Bulky) Leave a tail 8" (20.5cm) long at beginning then
work row as follows: *knit 1 stitch, purl 1 stitch; repeat
from * to last stitch, end row with knit 1.

ROW 2   (Sport-weight yarn—at the other end of the needle)
Slide stitches to other end of needle, pick up sport-
weight yarn and work as follows: *knit 1 stitch, purl 1
stitch; repeat from * to last stitch, end row with knit 1.

Repeat rows 1 and 2 until throw measures 54" (137cm), ending with
row 2. Bind off very loosely with sport-weight yarn (bind-off should
be as stretchable as knitting).

FINISHING

Soak throw in warm water for a few minutes. Then squeeze out as
much water as possible (or wrap throw in towel and squeeze towel to
remove excess water). Lay flat to dry, stretching throw to final size.

WRAP

After finishing the throw, I liked the design so much I decided to make a shawl using the same design—but this time I made the contrast between thick and thin yarn even greater. I teamed up the bulky yarn with lace.

Wrap is worked the long way. With bulky yarn, cast on 151 stitches. Break or cut bulky yarn leaving an 8" (20.5cm) yarn tail for fringe. Switch to lace- or fingering-weight yarn and work row 2 of stitch pattern (see KnitKnot Throw on previous page for stitch pattern instructions). Switch to bulky yarn and work row 1 of pattern. Continue in pattern, alternating between bulky and lace/fingering-weight yarns. Work in pattern until wrap measures about 22" (56cm), ending with row 2 of pattern. Switch to bulky yarn and bind off very loosely.

FINISHING

Soak shawl in warm water for a few minutes. Then squeeze out as much water as possible (or wrap shawl in towel and squeeze towel to remove excess water). Lay flat to dry, stretching shawl to final size.

ABOUT THE FRINGE

For the throw, I simply trimmed the fringe strands to even lengths. For the wrap, I tied 2 pieces of fringe together. Your choice—you don't have to decide until after you've washed and blocked the piece.

SIZE (after washing and blocking)
Width: 24" (61cm).
Length: 76" (193cm), not including fringe.

YARN
Bulky yarn, about 300 yards (229m), and lace- or fingering-weight yarn, about 250 yards (229m).

The sample is knit with Morehouse Merino Bulky in Cardinal Red, 3 skeins; and Lace, 2 skeins.

NEEDLES
Size 15 (10mm): 29" (73.5cm) circular needle (or longer).

OTHER MATERIALS
Tapestry needle.

GAUGE
About 10 stitches = 4 inches (10cm) in pattern. After washing and blocking, this pattern will expand widthwise—not much lengthwise— and the final gauge will be around 8 stitches = 4 inches (10cm).

Above: MaryPat wearing the KnitKnot Wrap in her favorite color, red.

Opposite: The bug patrol at the farm includes this pair of Guinea hens—unfortunately, their beat does not include our closets and drawers.

STORING WOOLENS

Nowadays, most commercially spun knitting yarn contains a mothproofing ingredient; however, frequent washing may weaken its effectiveness. To keep knitting yarn natural and chemical free, some yarns—Morehouse Merino included—contain no mothproofing at all. To be completely safe, with your woolens that is, follow the guidelines below.

Advice to wash your woolens before storing them to keep them safe from moths is probably based more on a desire for hygiene than on scientific evidence that moths prefer soiled sweaters to freshly laundered ones. I have tested moths' appetites (unwittingly, I might add) many times and found little proof of their preference for a pair of unwashed mittens over a brand-new skein of yarn.

Moths are able to find your sweater stash, supposedly, because they smell the sulphur, which is a component of wool. That's why strongly fragrant herbs are used as moth repellents—they disguise the smell of the wool and outwit the critters. But a large and hungry population of moths may not be fooled for long. And herbs don't get rid of the pests, they simply deter them, or so we hope. If you have an infestation of moths in your home, you may have to consider a more drastic approach: mothballs. The vapors from the mothballs are toxic to the bugs and will actually kill them.

Plastic bins with tight-fitting lids are the best place to store woolens. If the bins are too bulky for your closet, use plastic bags instead. One caveat: make sure the sweater is fully dry before packing it into a plastic bag. And don't pack a sweater away on a rainy day with the air full of moisture.

CHAPTER TWO

LACE

Knitting with lace yarn is habit forming. Twenty years ago when we spun our first merino wool into yarn, we made a sport-weight and a worsted-weight yarn. Then customers began asking for a lace- or fingering-weight yarn made with our soft merino wool.

At the time, I wondered, *who has time to knit with yarn that fine, using spindly needles, working for hours, and advancing by millimeters?* But we did spin some of our wool into lace, and it turned into an overnight success. Eventually, even I came around and tried my hand at lace knitting. I have not stopped since. The fine yarn and small needles are actually a treat after working with bulky yarn and pole-sized needles.

Now I enjoy designing new stitch variations for lace more than I do for any other projects—probably because lace yarn shows stitches more clearly than other yarn.

REED SHAWL
AND SCARF

Finding inspirations for lace designs in nature is as easy as a walk along a country road. With their soft colors and delicate blossoms, weeds, grasses, and wildflowers all supply an abundance of design ideas. The beige-brown colors and fine texture of the reed weed inspired this shawl.

SHAWL

> NOTE When switching yarn colors, don't break off yarn—let the previous color hang at the side of the shawl until you are ready to resume knitting with it again, then pull it up loosely to the beginning of the new row and continue with pattern.

With light color yarn, cast on 135 stitches. Knit 10 rows for garter stitch border. Then begin reed lace pattern.

REED LACE PATTERN

ROW 1   *Knit 1, yarn over needle (it does not matter whether you put yarn over needle from front to back or from back to front—whichever way works best for your style of knitting); repeat from * to last stitch, ending row with knit 1.

ROW 2   *Knit 1, drop yarn-over from previous row; repeat from * to last stitch, ending row with knit 1.

Drop light color and change to darker color yarn.

ROW 3   *Knit 1, with yarn in back slip next stitch as if to purl; repeat from * to last stitch, ending row with knit 1.

ROW 4   *Knit 1, purl 1; repeat from * to last stitch, ending row with knit 1.

Drop darker color and change to light color yarn.

SIZE
About 25" (63.5cm) wide and 74" (188cm) long, after washing and blocking.

YARN
Lace- or fingering-weight yarn in 2 tones, one light and one dark.
About 1,000 yards (914.5m) of the lighter color; 440 yards (402.5m) of the darker color.

The sample is knit with Morehouse Merino Lace in Natural Oatmeal and Natural Brown Heather; 5 skeins in light color and 2 skeins in darker color.

NEEDLES
Size 6 or 7 (4 or 4.5mm).

OTHER MATERIALS
Tapestry needle.

GAUGE
24 stitches = 4 inch (10cm) in pattern, before washing and blocking (but gauge is not crucial; if you knit tightly, use the larger size needle.)

Above: Blowing in the wind . . . the reeds behind the pond inspired this shawl.

Opposite: The Reed Shawl—a natural beauty.

The Reed Scarf with light and dark colors reversed.

SIZE (after washing and blocking)
Width: About 9" (23cm) wide.
Length: 60" (152.5cm). Measurements do not include fringe.

YARN
Lace- or fingering-weight yarn in 2 tones, one light and the other dark.
About 640 yards (585.5m) of the darker color; 200 yards (183m) of the lighter color.

The sample is knit with Morehouse Merino Lace in Natural Brown Heather and Natural Oatmeal; 3 skeins in dark color and 1 skein in light color.

NEEDLES
Size 6 or 7 (4 or 4.5mm).

OTHER MATERIALS
Tapestry needle.

GAUGE
24 stitches = 4 inches (10cm) in pattern (but gauge is not crucial; if you knit tightly, use the larger size needle.)

Opposite: Morehouse Farm on a cloudless spring day.

| ROW 5 | *Knit 1, with yarn in back slip next stitch as if to purl; repeat from * to last stitch, ending row with knit 1. |
| ROW 6 | *Knit 1, purl 1; repeat from * to last stitch, ending row with knit 1. |

Repeat these 6 rows until shawl measures about 72" to 73" (183 to 185.5cm). End shawl with light color yarn and knit 10 rows for garter stitch border. Bind off loosely. Weave in yarn tails.

FINISHING

Soak shawl in warm water for several minutes. Squeeze out as much water as possible (or roll shawl in towel and squeeze towel). Lay shawl flat to dry, stretching it to final size.

SCARF

With dark color, cast on 55 stitches. Knit 4 rows for garter stitch border.

Follow reed lace pattern for shawl, reversing light and dark colors and repeating rows 1 though 6. Work in pattern until scarf measures 59" (150cm). End scarf with dark color yarn and 4 knit rows for garter stitch border. Bind off loosely. Weave in yarn tails. Add fringe.

FINISHING

Soak scarf in warm water for several minutes. Squeeze out as much water as possible (or roll scarf or shawl in towel and squeeze towel). Lay scarf flat to dry, stretching it to final size.

HUCK LACE SHAWL

The idea for this shawl is borrowed from huck lace weaving patterns. I wanted to knit a shawl with the same beautiful open lacework a weaver creates on a loom.

Cast on 110 stitches and knit 36 rows.

Next, follow pattern sequences in order described in steps on page 43.

PATTERN SEQUENCE I

ROW 1   Knit 10 stitches, *knit into stitch 2 rows below but don't drop stitch off needle, knit the same stitch again (still on your left-hand needle) as a regular knit stitch, then slip the first stitch (now on your right-hand needle) over second stitch (as if to bind off); rep from * to last 10 stitches, knit these last 10 stitches.

ROW 2   Knit 10 stitches, purl row to last 10 stitches, knit these last 10 stitches.

ROW 3   Knit.

ROW 4   Repeat row 2.

PATTERN SEQUENCE II

ROW 1   Knit.

ROW 2   Knit 10 stitches, purl row to last 10 stitches, knit these last 10 stitches.

PATTERN SEQUENCE III

ROW 1   Knit 10 stitches, *knit into stitch 1 row below but don't drop stitch off the needle, knit the same stitch again as a regular stitch, then slip the first stitch (now on your right needle) over second stitch (as if to bind off); rep from * to last 10 stitches, knit these last 10 stitches.

SIZE
(before washing and blocking)
Width: 22" (56cm).
Length: About 80" (203cm).

(after washing and blocking)
Width: 27" (68.5cm).
Length: 84" (213.5cm).

YARN
Lace- or fingering-weight yarn, about 1,600 yards (1,463m).

The sample is knit with Morehouse Merino Lace in Natural White; 7 skeins.

NEEDLES
Size 5 or 6 (3.75 or 4mm).

OTHER MATERIALS
Tapestry needle.

GAUGE
About 20 stitches = 4 inches (10cm) in garter stitch, before washing and blocking.

KNIT INTO STITCH BELOW

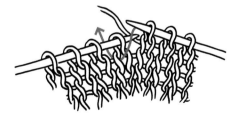

Opposite: The Huck Lace Shawl showing off its transparent beauty.

BLOCKING LACE, OR
TURNING THE UGLY DUCKLING INTO A SWAN

Usually when you finish a lace scarf or shawl, it has all the appeal of a dishrag. Turning the ugly duckling into a swan is the final step in lace knitting. The transformation takes place during the washing and blocking stage. Soak the shawl or scarf in warm water for a few minutes to relax and loosen the stitches. Then, squeeze out as much water as possible and lay it flat to dry on a large surface. A bed works well since its length is roughly equal to the length of the average shawl. Ideally, the fringe will hang over the edge of the bed. Fringe that hangs while drying will straighten nicely. Stretch the scarf or shawl to its final shape or size—I never use pins. If the scarf or shawl keeps returning to its original size, keep stretching until you win the battle and the garment stays put.

ROW 2	Knit 10 stitches, purl row to last 10 stitches, knit these last 10 stitches.

A close-up of the lovely open lacework that gives this shawl its character and beauty.

Step 1: Work Pattern Sequence I a total of 5 times (20 rows).

Step 2: Work Pattern Sequence II a total of 7 times (14 rows); then work Pattern Sequence III once (2 rows); work Pattern Sequence II a total of 7 times again (14 rows).

Step 3: Now work Pattern Sequence I a total of 4 times (16 rows).

Step 4: Repeat step 2 (30 rows).

Step 5: Work Pattern Sequence I a total of 3 times (12 rows).

Step 6: Repeat step 2 (30 rows).

Step 7: Work Pattern Sequence I a total of 2 times (8 rows).

Step 8: Repeat step 2 (30 rows).

Step 9: Work Pattern Sequence I once (4 rows).

Next, *work Pattern Sequence II 15 times (30 rows). Then work Pattern Sequence III once (2 rows)*.

Repeat from * to * 6 more times (192 rows).

Work Pattern Sequence II 15 times (30 rows).

Finish shawl with the same pattern sequence as it began, but in reverse order—starting with step 9, followed by 8, then 7 and so on down to the beginning. End shawl with 36 knit rows. Bind off loosely (bind-off should be as stretchy/elastic as knitting). Weave in yarn tails.

FINISHING

Soak the shawl in warm water for several minutes. Squeeze out as much water as possible (or roll in towel and squeeze towel). Lay the shawl flat to dry (on bed or other large surface) stretching it to its final size. There is no need to pin shawl, just stretch it to its full width and length.

Opposite: Flapping its wings will probably not turn this goose into a swan.

FOULARD WITH CASE

These little scarves will come to your rescue on hot summer days after you enter an air conditioned restaurant or movie theater and the cold, while refreshing at first, begins to bother you. The scarves are designed with a stitch size that will not wrinkle or crease easily, no matter how long or how tightly crammed the Foulard has been in its case. Just pull it out and shake it once or twice, and it will look as smooth as freshly blocked lace.

There are three sizes to choose from. The smallest makes a handy head-cover if a sudden breeze threatens to upset your coif; the largest can serve as a sarong. The case will keep the Foulard safely stored in your purse until the next movie, dinner, or wind gust.

FOULARD

NOTE Foulards are knit from corner to corner.

INCREASING ROWS

Cast on 3 stitches and knit one row.

Knit into the front and back of the first stitch, then knit to end of row. Continue increasing like this until you have 100 stitches on the needle for the small size, 125 stitches for the medium size, or 150 stitches for the large size. Knit 2 rows.

DECREASING ROWS

Knit across row to last 2 stitches, knit these 2 stitches together. Continue decreasing like this until you have 3 stitches left. Bind off.

FINISHING

Weave in yarn ends. Wash Foulard in warm water. Squeeze out as much water as possible (or roll in towel and squeeze towel). Lay flat to dry, stretching it to final size.

Above: Another way to use the Foulard: heading back to the cabana from the beach.

Opposite: Light dressing—absolutely no calories.

SIZES (after washing and blocking)
Small: 32" x 32" (81cm x 81cm). Medium: 40" x 40" (101.5cm x 101.5cm). Large: 50" x 50" (127cm x 127cm).

YARN
Lace- or fingering-weight yarn, about 440 yards (402.5m) for small size, 660 yards (603.5m) for medium, and 880 yards (805m) for large.

The samples are knit with Variegated Morehouse Merino Lace. Use a double skein for the small size, triple skein for the medium, and a quad skein for large size.

NEEDLES
Size 11 (8mm).

OTHER MATERIALS
Tapestry needle.

GAUGE
Not crucial, about 12 stitches = 4 inches (10 cm) in garter stitch, before washing and blocking.

SIZES

Envelope-style: 8½" (22cm) wide.
Tall pocket-style: 7" (18cm) wide.

YARN

Lace- or fingering-weight yarn, about 200 yards (183m). Use leftover yarn from Foulard or other odds and ends.

The samples are knit with Morehouse Merino Lace and use 1 skein each.

NEEDLES

Size 2 (2.75mm).

OTHER MATERIALS

One decorative button; tapestry needle.

GAUGE

25 stitches = 4 inches (10cm) in garter stitch.

Three Foulard Cases in different color combinations. And check out the buttons: a doggie face, a mouse with a tail, and a sheep with dangling feet.

FOULARD CASE

For the envelope-style case, cast on 54 stitches; for pocket-style case, 45 stitches. Knit until piece measures 10" (25.5cm) for the envelope-style; and 7½" (19cm) for the pocket-style.

ALL STYLES

Knit 8 more rows, then start decreases for flap.

DECREASE ROW Knit row to last 2 stitches, knit these 2 stitches together. Repeat this row until you have 24 stitches on the needle.

BUTTONHOLE ROW Knit 10 stitches, bind off next 3 stitches (for buttonhole), then knit to last 2 stitches, knit these 2 stitches together.

NEXT ROW Knit to where you bound off for buttonhole and cast on 3 stitches (use e-loop cast-on, see illustration below), then knit to last 2 stitches, knit these 2 stitches together.

Continue with decreases—knit each row to last 2 stitches and knit these 2 stitches together—until you have 10 stitches left. Bind off.

FINISHING

Fold over case to ½" (1.3cm) before decreases begin for flap and sew the side edges together. Attach button to align with buttonhole. Weave in yarn ends.

E-LOOP CAST ON

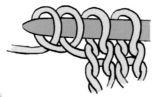

Why hide the Foulard inside the bag? Create a colorful accent by tying it to the straps of your handbag.

RABBIT-PROOF SCARF

Not a rabbit-proof fence, but it is chicken proof.

The Rabbit-Proof Fence runs across Australia, keeping the rabbits on one side, and the livestock and land under cultivation on the other. A movie by the same name tells the story of three Aboriginal girls who find their way back home by walking along this fence for hundreds of miles. It's a true story, and one of my favorite films. This scarf design developed as I watched the movie. By picking up stitches and then unraveling them a few rows later, I've let the rabbits slip through the gaps in my fence.

Cast on 49 stitches and knit 20 rows then start with pattern.

SIZE
8" (20.5cm) wide—to desired length.

YARN
Lace- or fingering-weight yarn, about 500 yards (457m).

The sample is knit with Morehouse Merino Lace in Periwinkle; 3 skeins.

NEEDLES
Size 4 or 5 (3.5 or 3.75mm).

OTHER MATERIALS
Tapestry needle.

GAUGE
24 stitches = 4 inches (10cm) in garter stitch, before washing and blocking.

STITCH PATTERN

ROW 1	Knit 3 stitches, *drop 1 stitch (drop it off the needle—then later pull the dropped stitch down to cast-on), knit 6 stitches; repeat from * to last 4 stitches, drop the next stitch, and knit the last 3 stitches.
ROWS 2–4	Knit.
ROW 5	*Knit 6 stitches, increase 1 stitch (increase by picking up yarn between stitches with left-hand needle and knitting the loop—the hole this creates in the row below doesn't matter, because the stitch will be dropped and unraveled a few rows later); repeat from * to end of row, ending row with knit 6 stitches.
ROWS 6–14	Knit.
ROW 15	*Knit 6 stitches, drop next stitch off needle; repeat from * to last 6 stitches, ending row with knit 6 stitches.
ROWS 16–18	Knit.
ROW 19	Knit 3 stitches, *increase 1 stitch (work increase as before—by picking up yarn between stitches and knitting the loop), knit 6 stitches; repeat from * to last 3 stitches, end row with increase 1 stitch, knit 3 stitches.

ROWS 20–38 Knit.

Repeat this pattern sequence, beginning with row 1, to desired length of scarf or shawl, ending with row 38 of pattern, then work first row of pattern. Bind off loosely.

FINISHING

Weave in yarn tails. Soak scarf in warm water for a few minutes. Squeeze out as much water as possible (or roll scarf in towel and squeeze towel). Lay flat to dry, stretching it to its final size. There is no need to pin it, just stretching it thoroughly will be enough.

The Rabbit-Proof Scarf caught in the fence.

SPIRAL-RUFFLE SCARF

SIZE
About 3" (7.5cm) wide and 52" (132cm) long.

YARN
Variegated Lace- or fingering-weight yarn, 300 yards (274.5m); plus about 15 yards (14m) in a contrasting color for the bind-off row.

The sample is knit with Variegated Morehouse Merino Lace in Peacock; 1 double skein, plus small amount of white lace yarn for bind-off row.

NEEDLES
Size 6 (4mm).

OTHER MATERIALS
Tapestry needle.

GAUGE
About 20 stitches = 4 inches (10cm) in garter stitch pattern, before washing and blocking.

A peacock feather was the inspiration for the colors of the scarf.

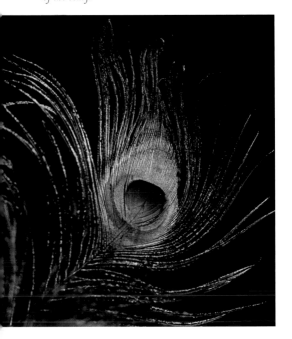

This pretty accessory charms a plain blouse into a Victorian fantasy. If you love ruffles, this design will definitely tickle your fancy. You might even try varying this pattern by using sport-weight yarn and, rather than stopping the increases at 17 stitches, keep going and turn the scarf into a shawl. Below is the pattern for the narrow, lacy version pictured.

Using yarn doubled (2 strands held together as one), cast on 50 stitches. Knit first row with yarn doubled.

NEXT 2 ROWS Continue work with single yarn and divide each double-yarn stitch into 2 by using 1 strand of yarn for 1 stitch, and the second strand for a second stitch—total of 100 stitches. Knit next row.

Begin pattern:

ROW 1 *Knit 5 stitches, knit next stitch and increase as follows: knit stitch but don't drop it off the left-hand needle, knit into back of the same stitch again; repeat from * to last 4 stitches, ending row with knit 4.

ROW 2 Knit.

ROW 3 *Knit 6 stitches, knit next stitch and increase 1 (same way as in row 1); repeat from * to last 4 stitches, ending row with knit 4.

ROW 4 Knit.

ROW 5 *Knit 7 stitches, knit next stitch and increase 1; repeat from * to last 4 stitches, ending row with knit 4.

ROW 6 Knit.

ROW 7 *Knit 8 stitches, knit next stitch and increase 1; repeat from * to last 4 stitches, ending with knit 4.

ROW 8 Knit.

ROW 9	*Knit 9 stitches, knit next stitch and increase 1; repeat from * to last 4 stitches, ending with knit 4.
ROW 10	Knit.
ROW 11	*Knit 10 stitches, knit next stitch and increase 1; repeat from * to last 4 stitches, ending with knit 4.
ROW 12	Knit.
ROW 13	*Knit 11 stitches, knit next stitch and increase 1; repeat from * to last 4 stitches, ending with knit 4.
ROW 14	Knit.
ROW 15	*Knit 12 stitches, knit next stitch and increase 1; repeat from * to last 4 stitches, ending with knit 4.
ROW16	Knit.
ROW 17	*Knit 13 stitches, knit next stitch and increase 1; repeat from * to last 4 stitches, ending with knit 4.
ROW 18	Knit.
ROW 19	*Knit 14 stitches, knit next stitch and increase 1; repeat from * to last 4 stitches, ending with knit 4.
ROW 20	Knit.
ROW 21	*Knit 15 stitches, knit next stitch and increase 1; repeat from * to last 4 stitches, ending with knit 4.
ROW 22	Knit.
ROW 23	*Knit 16 stitches, knit next stitch and increase 1; repeat from * to last 4 stitches, ending with knit 4.
ROW 24	Knit.
NEXT ROW	Switch to yarn in contrasting color and bind off very loosely.

Ruffles knit in variegated lace yarn.

FINISHING

Weave in yarn tails. Soak the scarf in warm water for several minutes. Squeeze out as much water as possible (or roll the scarf in a towel and squeeze the towel). When blocking this scarf, lay it in a circle with one layer on top of the other. Stretch each layer widthwise as far as it will stretch, then place the next spiral on top and stretch. Continue in this manner until all layers are blocked.

CHAPTER THREE

CHILDREN

Knitting for children offers instant gratification. Little hands, little feet, small bodies—all are easy to cover with just a few stitches and rows. Fit and style are simple and easy, and the colors to knit with will brighten the corner you sit in while clicking away. If the children join in, it's twice the fun. Short little scarves are a good way to introduce a child to knitting—the prospect of adding zany fringe at the end will get the project finished a lot faster.

It has been my observation that anything in the shape of animals, especially a creepy, crawly animal that we grown-ups detest, is a great hit with kids.

BUGGY MITTS
AND HATS

SIZES
Child's small (medium, large).
Length: 5 (6, 7)" [12.5 (15, 18) cm].

YARN
Small amounts of worsted-weight yarn,
approximately 150 yards (137m) total per pair
in lots of different colors—bugs come in a
variety of colors and color combinations.

The samples are knit with Morehouse Merino
3-Strand.

NEEDLES
Size 4 or 5 (3.5 or 3.75mm); set of 4 or 5
double-pointed. Adjust needle size if necessary to obtain correct gauge.

OTHER MATERIALS
Size C/2 or D/3 (2.75 or 3.25mm) crochet
hook to make antennae; felt and small beads
for eyes; tapestry needle; stitch markers;
stitch holder.

GAUGE
20 stitches = 4 inches (10 cm) in stockinette
stitch.

*Opposite: Isabella holding a black lamb in her
Buggy Mitts. In the background, the lamb's mom is
keeping an eye on the goings-on.*

For this basic children's mitten pattern, odds and ends of yarn and a
child fascinated by bugs are all you need to have some good knitting
fun. Use stockinette stitch for a bug with a slithery-smooth body,
seed stitch for bugs with bumps and lumps, or a single purl round for
the ones with ridges. Bugs are colorful, so use up leftover pieces of
bright yarn too small for other projects. Don't worry about darning in
yarn ends; just tie them together on the inside of the mitts and leave
½" (1.3cm) tails. These little tufts will make the mittens warmer and
cozier. The buggy mittens really come to life when you add a pair of
felt eyes with a tiny bead in the center and a pair of crochet antennae.
It's enough to make you fall in love with bugs.

MITTS

Cast on 26 (30, 34) stitches. Divide stitches evenly between needles.
Join and place marker to indicate beginning of rounds. Knit 15 (16,
18) rounds or desired length for cuff. If you want to roll up edge of
cuff, add another 10 rounds. Add stripes in different yarn colors or
work some rounds in purl instead of knit stitch (see samples on page
56 for ideas on how to combine colors and patterns).

THUMB GUSSET

Knit 1 stitch, place first marker, increase 1 (increase by picking up
yarn between stitches and knit into back of loop, so stitch appears to
be twisted), knit 1, increase 1, place second marker, knit to end of
round. Knit 2 rounds. Repeat these three rounds—increasing in first
round after first and before second marker—until you have 7 (9, 11)
stitches between markers. End thumb gusset with knit 2 rounds.

NEXT ROUND Knit 1, place next 7 (9, 11) stitches on holder (a paper clip will do nicely), knit to end of round—pull yarn tight after that first stitch to avoid a gap where stitches were placed on the holder. You now have 25 (29, 33) stitches.

Knit 12 (15, 18) rounds.

Even the wheels on this old tractor look buggy-eyed.

TOP SHAPING

DECREASE ROUND 1   *Knit 3 stitches, knit 2 together; repeat from * to end of round, ending with knit 0 (4, 3) stitches. Knit 3 rounds.

DECREASE ROUND 2   *Knit 2 stitches, knit 2 together; repeat from * to end of round, ending with knit 0 (4, 3) stitches. Knit 2 rounds.

DECREASE ROUND 3   *Knit 1 stitch, knit 2 together; repeat from * to end of round, ending with knit 0 (1, 0) stitch. Knit 1 round.

DECREASE ROUND 4   *Knit 2 together; repeat from * to end of round. Cut yarn leaving a 6" tail. Thread tail into tapestry needle, then draw yarn through remaining stitches. Weave in yarn tail.

THUMB

Put stitches from holder on 3 needles. Pick up 3 stitches between first and last stitch. You now have 10 (12, 14) stitches. Knit 10 (12, 14) rounds.

DECREASES *Knit 2 together; repeat from * to end of round. Draw yarn through remaining stitches as before.

FINISHING

Add the bug antennae to the tips of the mitts: with crochet hook and 2 strands of yarn held together as one, work crochet chain for 1" (2.5cm) to make the feelers. You can also crochet them right onto mitten by inserting crochet hook at tip of mitts, then pulling yarn loop through as your first chain stitch. Add felt eyes with tiny, shiny beads in the middle.

Opposite: Naming the bug will be the task of the recipient of these colorful mitts.

SIZES

Child's small (medium, large).
To fit 2- to 3-year-old (4- to 6-,
7- to 8-year-old).

YARN

150 yards (137m) of worsted-weight yarn in
same colors as Buggy Mitts.

The samples are knit with Morehouse Merino
3-Strand; 1 skein per hat.

NEEDLES

Size 5 or 6 (3.75 or 4mm); set of double-
pointed. Adjust needle size if necessary to
obtain correct gauge.

OTHER MATERIALS

Tapestry needle.

GAUGE

19 stitches = 4 inches (10cm) in stockinette
stitch pattern.

Cast on 72 (76, 80) stitches. Divide stitches evenly between needles. Join stitches into circle and knit 28 (32, 36) rounds. If you want to match mittens closely, include stripes in same colors.

FIRST DECREASE — *Knit 7 stitches, knit 2 stitches together; repeat from * to end of round (knit remaining stitches, if any, at the end of the round). Knit 5 rounds.

SECOND DECREASE — *Knit 6 stitches, knit 2 together; repeat from * to end of round. Knit 5 rounds.

THIRD DECREASE — *Knit 5, knit 2 together; repeat from * to end of round. Knit 5 rounds.

FOURTH DECREASE — *Knit 4, knit 2 together; repeat from * to end of round. Knit 5 rounds.

FIFTH DECREASE — *Knit 3, knit 2 together; repeat from * to end of round. Knit 5 rounds.

SIXTH DECREASE — *Knit 2, knit 2 together; repeat from * to end of round. Knit 5 rounds.

SEVENTH DECREASE — *Knit 1, knit 2 together; repeat from * to end round. Knit 5 rounds.

EIGHTH DECREASE — *Knit 2 together repeat from * to end of round. For large size hat only, repeat this last round once more.

NINTH DECREASE — *Knit 1, knit 2 together; repeat from * to end of round.

You should end up with 5 to 7 stitches at this point. Divide stitches evenly between 2 needles.

FINISHING

Switch to different color yarn and with the remaining stitches knit a cord about 5" (12.5cm) long. Cut yarn leaving a tail. Thread tail in tapestry needle, then draw yarn through stitches. Weave in yarn tails. Tie knot in cord.

HOW TO WASH WOOL

When washing wool (or laundry, for that matter) it is important to have some knowledge about soaps and detergents and to understand what happens in the washing process.

The cleaning action works like this: Soap added to the washing water attaches itself to soil particles, breaks the soil free from the garment (or the dishes in the dishwasher), then holds the soil particles in suspension in the water until rinsed away. That is why it is important not to overcrowd the washtub; if you do, the loosened soil particles will redeposit themselves on the garment because there is no room for them to float in the water.

Soaps are made from the fatty acids in fats and oils (from animal or plant sources). A strong alkali (caustic soda for heavy-duty detergents or caustic potash for mild hand soaps) is added to neutralize the acids. To this mix, the soap manufacturer adds a surface-active agent called a surfactant. Surfactants break down the surface tension (beading) of water, making it more "liquid" so it can spread more easily and penetrate garments.

There are many different types of soaps and detergents. They will determine the pH level of your washing water. The pH level is a measurement of the acidity or alkalinity of a solution. The pH scale runs from acid at 1 to alkali at 14. This is important to know, because acidic water will damage cotton, ramie, and linen (cellulose fibers from plants) and strong alkaline washing water will damage wool, cashmere, mohair, angora, and silk (protein fibers from animals). Battery acid will burn a hole in your overalls and bleach will devour wool (put a yard of knitting wool in a glass of bleach and put it aside for a few hours—the wool will disappear).

Mild soaps have a pH level of around 7, called a neutral pH—not too acidic and not too alkaline. Strong cleaning solutions will have a pH level of about 10 and are considered alkaline. Vinegar has a pH of about 3.

So how are we going to wash our woolens without doing a litmus test on each soap? (Litmus paper strips submerged in soapy water turn a different color depending on whether the water is acidic or alkaline.) Wool is best washed with soaps with a neutral pH. Dishwashing liquids and detergents that the manufacturer claims are gentle on your hands have neutral pH levels (our skin is also affected by strong alkali). Strong detergents are not suitable for wool because they are too alkaline and could damage fibers (the more cleaning action a product promises, the more alkaline it will be). Soaps made specifically for washing woolens have a pH level in the neutral range.

Increasing the temperature of the water will also increase the level of acidity or alkalinity, which will make the cleaning action of the soap or detergent stronger. So if your are not sure about a soap's pH level, using warm water instead of hot will lessen the chance of damage.

Blends of yarn (cotton with wool, or ramie with alpaca for instance) may create special washing problems: wool needs low alkalinity but can tolerate acidic soap, and with cotton it's just the opposite. Use a mild soap (or follow the manufacturer's washing recommendations) and warm water.

I've successfully used Palmolive dishwashing liquid (the green stuff) on my woolens for about twenty years. The original version is my favorite. Unfortunately, the manufacturer keeps changing its formula, including the color.

CHILD'S SWEATER WITH MATCHING HAT

Bright and happy yarn colors will result in a pair of warm and happy kids. Bulky yarn makes this one a project with the end in clear sight. And, as you can see, the sheep approve.

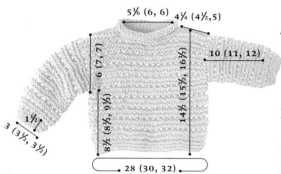

5⅙ (6, 6)   4¼ (4½, 5)

6 (7, 7)

10 (11, 12)

14½ (15½, 16½)

1½

8½ (8½, 9½)

3 (3½, 3½)

28 (30, 32)

SWEATER

> NOTE This sweater is worked in the round using circular needles. The sleeves are knit in the round and worked onto the sweater by picking up stitches around the armhole openings.

STITCH PATTERN (WORKED IN THE ROUND FOR BODY)

ROUND 1 (MAIN COLOR)	Purl.
ROUND 2 (MAIN COLOR)	Knit.
ROUND 3 (MAIN COLOR)	Purl.
ROUND 4 (MAIN COLOR)	Knit.
ROUND 5 (CONTRAST COLOR)	*Knit 1, slip stitch as if to purl with yarn in back; rep from * to end of round. Break off yarn after finishing round, leaving a tail just long enough to tie together with piece at beginning of round.
ROUND 6 (MAIN COLOR)	*Slip stitch as if to purl with yarn in back, knit 1; rep from * to end of round.
ROUND 7 (MAIN COLOR)	Knit.

These 7 rounds constitute stitch pattern for body of sweater (including sleeves).

SIZES
Child's size 4 (6, 8).

YARN
Bulky yarn, about 410 (410, 510) yards [375 (375, 466) m] in main color; about 80 yards (73m) in contrasting color.

The samples are knit with Morehouse Merino Bulky in Royal with Sunflower Yellow and in Moss with Geranium; 4 (5, 8) skeins, plus 1 additional skein in contrasting color.

NEEDLES
Size 11 (8mm): 24" (61cm) long; set of 4 or 5 double-pointed needles for neck and sleeves. Spare circular needles for holding stitches. Adjust needle size if necessary to obtain correct gauge.

OTHER MATERIALS
Tapestry needle.

GAUGE
11 stitches = 4 inches (10cm) in garter stitch pattern.

Opposite: Isabella tucking in her brother's shirt.

STITCH PATTERN
(WORKED BACK AND FORTH FOR FRONT AND
BACK AFTER ARMHOLE DIVISION)

ROW 1 (MAIN COLOR, WRONG SIDE)   Knit.

ROW 2 (MAIN COLOR)   Knit.

ROW 3 (MAIN COLOR)   Knit.

ROW 4 (MAIN COLOR)   Knit.

ROW 5 (CONTRASTING COLOR, WS)   *Purl 1, slip 1 stitch as if to purl with yarn in front; repeat from * to end of row, ending with purl 1 (sizes 6 & 8: *slip 1 stitch as if to purl with yarn in front, purl 1; repeat from * to end of row).

Slide stitches back to other end of needle where main color yarn is waiting.

ROW 6 (MAIN COLOR, WRONG SIDE)   *Slip 1 as if to purl with yarn in front, purl 1; repeat from * to end of row, ending with slip 1 (sizes 6 & 8: *purl 1, slip 1 stitch as if to purl with yarn in front, repeat from * to end of row).

ROW 7 (MAIN COLOR, RIGHT SIDE)   Knit.

BODY

Cast on 74 (80, 84) stitches. Place marker for beginning of round and join. [Purl 1 round. Knit 1 round] 3 times—total of 6 rounds. Knit next round as follows: *increase 1 stitch, knit 18 (20, 21) stitches; repeat from * to end of round (on size 4, knit last 2 stitches). You now have 78 (84, 88) stitches. Start with round 5 of pattern.

Repeat pattern until you have 6 (6, 7) rounds with the contrasting color, ending with round 6 of pattern.

DIVIDE FOR ARMHOLES

Knit the first 39 (42, 44) stitches for the back piece; place the remaining 39 (42, 44) for the front on spare needle.

BACK

Continue working back piece. You'll be working rows back and forth now. Begin with row 1 of pattern and work in pattern until you have 4 (5, 5) rows with the contrasting color, ending with row 4 of pattern.

LAMBING TIME

One bitter cold January night, a young, inexperienced ewe was getting ready to lamb. I was worried about the lamb's chances for survival, so I stayed up waiting for it to arrive. It was getting late, so I finally got my sleeping bag and lay down in the straw next to the expectant ewe and promptly fell asleep. When I woke up, there was a lamb, already up and happily wagging its tail while nursing away.

The scene reminded me of a cartoon I once saw in which a farmer stands next to an expectant ewe, thinking, "I wish she would lamb so I could go back to bed." Meanwhile, the ewe is thinking, "I wish he would go back to bed so I could lamb."

Break off main color yarn, leaving about 20" (51cm) to work shoulder bind-off. Put stitches on spare needle for holding.

FRONT

Slip front stitches from spare needle to working needle. Work to same length as back piece. Now bind off shoulders from front and back piece together, using three-needle bind-off as follows: Put needles from front and back piece parallel to each other—with wrong side of sweater facing out. Starting at shoulder and working towards neck, knit the first stitch on needle closest to you together with first stitch on needle in back, then knit second stitch on needle closest to you together with second one on needle in back, then bind off in the usual manner by lifting first stitch over second one. Continue this way, knitting two stitches together from front and back needle, then binding off. Bind off 12 (13, 14) stitches at each shoulder. The remaining stitches are the neck stitches—15 (16, 16) stitches each on front and back.

ROLL NECK

Using double-pointed needles, knit stitches around neck opening. At each shoulder, pick up 1 additional stitch—total of 32 (34, 34) stitches. Knit 6 rounds, then bind-off very loosely.

SLEEVES

Using double-pointed needles, pick up 32 (38, 38) stitches around sleeve opening as follows: with right side facing and starting at armhole division, pick up 1 stitch per 2 rows. Pick up 1 additional stitch at shoulder and 1 additional stitch at underarm position. Start with round 1 of pattern and work in pattern until sleeve measures about 10 (11, 12)" [25.5 (28, 30.5) cm] ending with round 6 of pattern. If neeeded to achieve proper length, repeat round 6 of pattern.

DECREASE *Purl 2 stitches together; rep from * to end of round.

CUFF *Knit 1 round, purl 1 round; rep from * 3 times. Bind off very loosely in last purl round.

Repeat for other sleeve. Weave in ends.

MATCHING HAT

Cast on 48 (50) stitches. Place marker for beginning of round and join. [Purl 1 round. Knit 1 round] 4 times—8 rounds total.

Start with round 5 of sweater pattern and work to round 4. Knit 10 (12) rounds.

FIRST DECREASE	*Knit 4 stitches, knit 2 stitches together*; repeat from * to end of round (on larger size hat, knit the last 2 stitches). Knit 3 rounds.
SECOND DECREASE	*Knit 3 stitches, knit 2 stitches together; rep from * to end of round. Knit 2 rounds.
THIRD DECREASE	*Knit 2 stitches, knit 2 stitches together; rep from * to end of round. Knit 1 round.
FOURTH DECREASE	*Knit 1 stitch, knit 2 stitches together; rep from * to end of round.
FIFTH DECREASE	*Knit 2 stitches together; rep from * to end of round. Pull yarn through remaining stitches. Weave in ends.

FINISHING

Crochet or braid 2-pieces of cord between 3" and 4" (7.5 and 10cm) long. Make 2 pom-poms (see page 101) and attach to cords, then attach cords to top of hat.

SIZES
Child's size 2- to 4-year-old (5- to 8-year-old).

YARN
Bulky yarn, about 100 yards (91m) in main color; 1½ yards (1.4m) of bulky yarn in contrasting color (or use a piece of left-over worsted-weight-yarn doubled); small amount of yarn for pom-poms.

Samples are knit with Morehouse Merino Bulky; 1 skein per hat plus small amount in contrasting color.

NEEDLES
Size 10 or 11 (6.5 or 8mm); set of 5 double-pointed. Adjust needle size if necessary to obtain correct gauge.

OTHER MATERIALS
Tapestry needle.

GAUGE
12 stitches = 4 inches (10cm) in stockinette stitch pattern. (The hat gauge is a little tighter than sweater gauge.)

Above: A pair of hats to match the sweaters.

MOLLY'S JACKET, TURTLENECK, AND HAT

This is an outfit that pulled itself together. First, I knit the jacket with variegated bulky yarn in Molly's favorite colors. Then, I discovered some yarn leftover from another project in just the right shade for the turtleneck shell. And Molly added the hat (because it was cold that afternoon).

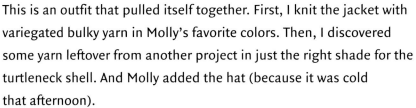

4 (4¼, 4¾, 5¼)   5 (5½, 5½, 6)
2½ (2¾, 3, 3)
7 (7½, 8, 8½)
16 (17, 18, 19)
10 (11, 12, 13)
3 TO 3½
26 (28, 30, 33)

JACKET

> NOTE This jacket is knit in one piece. There are no borders on left and right front; the buttonholes are worked as you are knitting the jacket. Knit the edge stitches tightly, so the selvedges will be firm and neat looking. The sleeves are knit in the round and are worked onto jacket by picking up stitches around armhole openings.

SEED STITCH PATTERN (WORKED OVER ODD NUMBER OF STITCHES)

*Knit 1 stitch, purl 1 stitch; repeat from * to last stitch, ending row with knit 1. Repeat this row for pattern.

BODY

Cast on 83 (89, 95, 103) stitches. Work 16 (20, 24, 28) rows in pattern. Next, work buttonhole as follows: work 2 stitches in pattern, purl 2 stitches together, continue in pattern (starting with a knit stitch) to end of row; turn and work next row in pattern to last 3 stitches, purl next stitch but before dropping stitch off the left-hand needle, knit into back of the stitch once more, work last 2 stitches in pattern. Work 16 rows in pattern and repeat the 2 rows for second buttonhole. Work 8 (8, 8, 6) more rows.

SIZES
Child's size 4 (6, 8 and 10).

YARN
Bulky yarn, 450 yards (400.5m) for sizes 4, 6, and 8; 550 yards (503m) for size 10.

The sample is knit with Morehouse Variegated Bulky in Zest; 4 skeins for sizes 4, 6, and 8; 5 skeins for size 10.

NEEDLES
Size 10½ or 11 (6.5 or 8mm), 29" (73.5cm) circular, or longer; set of 4 or 5 double-pointed, same size, for sleeves. Spare circular needles to use as stitch holders. Adjust needle size if necessary to obtain correct gauge.

OTHER MATERIALS
Four buttons; tapestry needle.

GAUGE
12 stitches and 20 rows = 4 inches (10cm) in seed stitch pattern.

Opposite: Molly feeding feathery friends.

Feathers on the frozen pond.

RIGHT FRONT

Work 21 (23, 25, 27) stitches in pattern. Put the remaining stitches on a spare needle for holder, turn and work in pattern back to beginning of row. Continue on right front and when you have worked a total of 16 rows from last buttonhole, repeat the 2 rows for third buttonhole. Work 14 more rows in pattern. Start neck decreases; the last buttonhole will be worked in the border around neck.

NECK DECREASES

Bind off at beginning of right side rows as follows—4 stitches 1 time, 2 stitches 2 (3, 3, 4) times, 1 stitch 1 (0, 1, 0) time(s), then work 4 (6, 6, 6) more rows even in pattern. You now have a total of 12 (13, 14, 15) stitches remaining. Put these stitches on a spare holding needle.

LEFT FRONT

Slip the 21 (23, 25, 27) stitches at the left side of the first spare needle to the working needle and repeat from armhole division for left front, reversing neck shaping.

BACK

Slip the back stitches from the spare needle to the working needle and work in pattern to same length as the two fronts. Now bind off shoulders together using three-needle bind-off as follows: With the wrong side of the jacket facing out, align stitches from the front and back pieces parallel to each other.

Starting at the shoulder and working towards neck, knit the first stitch on needle closest to you together with first stitch on needle in back, then knit second stitch on needle closest to you together with second one on needle in back, then bind off in the usual manner by lifting first stitch over second one. Continue this way, knitting two stitches together from front and back needle, then binding off. Bind off 12 (13, 14, 15) stitches from each shoulder. The remaining stitches are for the back neck.

NECK BORDER

Pick up stitches around neckline decreases as follows: With right side facing out and starting at right front, pick up 1 stitch per stitch on the neck bind-off and decreases, then pick up 1 stitch per 2 rows (where you worked straight rows after neckline decreases), then pick up 1 stitch at shoulder, knit the stitches from back piece, pick up an additional stitch at shoulder again, and pick up stitches on left front in the same manner as on right front. Work first row in seed stitch pattern and at each shoulder knit 2 stitches together (or purl 2 stitches together, if pattern calls for a purl stitch as the next stitch)

BUTTONHOLE ROWS	Work in seed stitch pattern and add fourth buttonhole.
BORDER	Work 2 more rows in seed stitch pattern. Bind off.

SLEEVES

With double-pointed needles, pick up stitches around armhole opening as follows: Starting at underarm location and with right side facing out, pick up 1 stitch per 2 rows along armhole. Pick up 1 additional stitch at shoulder. You will have a total of 37 (39, 41, 43) stitches. Make sure you have an odd number of stitches so seed stitch pattern appears uninterrupted at beginning and end of round. Place a marker at the beginning of the round.

SEED STITCH PATTERN
(WORKED IN THE ROUND)

ROUND 1	*Knit 1 stitch, purl 1 stitch; repeat from* to last stitch, ending round with knit 1.
ROUND 2	*Purl 1 stitch, knit 1 stitch; repeat from * to last stitch, ending round with purl 1.

Work 5 rounds even in pattern. Then work decreases in round 6 as follows: Knit first 2 stitches together, work round in pattern to last 2 stitches, knit these 2 stitches together. Continue in pattern, beginning with round 2 of pattern (to adjust pattern for decreases). *Work 5 rounds in pattern and then repeat decrease round (6 rounds total); repeat from * to final sleeve length—about 10 (11, 12, 13)" [25.5 (28, 30.5, 33) cm] long. Repeat for other sleeve.

A rooster gets all of Molly's attention.

SIZES
Child's size 4 (6, 8, 10).

YARN
Bulky yarn, 300—400 yards (274.5—366m); or worsted-weight yarn used doubled, 450-550 yards (411.5-503m).

The sample is knit with 2 strands of Morehouse 3-Strand held together as one in Denim; 3 skeins for sizes 4 and 6; 4 skeins for sizes 8 and 10.

NEEDLES
Size 11 or 13 (8 or 9mm): 24" (61cm) long; set of double-pointed, same size, for turtleneck; spare needle to use as stitch holder. Adjust needle size if necessary to obtain correct gauge.

OTHER MATERIALS
Tapestry needle.

GAUGE
10 stitches and 16 rows = 4 inches (10cm) in stockinette stitch pattern.

POCKETS (MAKE TWO)

Cast on 13 stitches and work 20 rows in seed stitch pattern. Bind off. Sew on jacket about 1" (2.5cm) from bottom border and 3" to 4" (7.5 to 10cm) in from left and right front.

TURTLENECK

BODY

Cast on 62 (66, 70, 72) stitches. Place marker and join. Knit until piece measures 8 (9, 10, 11)" [20.5 (23, 25.5, 28) cm].

DIVIDE FOR ARMHOLES Knit first 2 stitches together, knit 29 (31, 33, 34) stitches and place remaining stitches on spare needle for holder. Turn and (on wrong side) knit the first 2 stitches together, knit next stitch, then purl to last 2 stitches, knit these 2 stitches. Turn and knit the first 2 stitches together, knit to end of row. Turn and knit the first 2 stitches together, knit next stitch, then purl to last 2 stitches, knit these 2 stitches—you'll have 27 (29, 31, 32) stitches left. Continue working on front as follows: knit on right side rows; on wrong-side rows, knit the first 2 stitches, purl across the row to last 2 stitches, and knit the last 2 stitches. Work until piece measures 3½ (4, 4½, 4½)" [9 (10, 11.5, 11.5) cm] from armhole division.

NECK SHAPING

Knit 11 (11, 12, 12) stitches. Turn and slip first stitch (with yarn in front), purl next stitch and pass slipped stitch over purl stitch; purl row to last 2 stitches, knit 2 stitches.

SHORT ROWS   Knit 10 (10, 11, 11) stitches. Repeat decrease row on the wrong side.

Next, knit 9 (9, 10, 10) stitches, then repeat decrease row. Leave a piece 15" (38cm) long for binding off shoulder later. Put stitches on a holding needle and repeat neck decreases for right front, beginning first row at armhole edge at other end of front piece. The decreases will be on right side row, so when you slip stitch, slip stitch with yarn in back.

BACK

Slip back stitches to working needle, repeat armhole decreases, and work in same manner to same length as front pieces. Now bind off shoulder stitches together using three-needle bind-off. Align front and back pieces parallel to each other—wrong side facing out—and, starting at shoulders, knit first stitch on needle closest to you together with first stitch on needle in back, then knit second stitch on needle closest to you together with second stitch on needle in back, then bind off in the usual manner by lifting first stitch over second one. Bind off both shoulders. What you'll have left are stitches on back and middle stitches on front at beginning of neck decreases.

TURTLENECK

With double-pointed needles, pick up stitches around neck as follows: Starting at left shoulder with right side facing out, pick up 1 stitch before each decrease and 1 stitch at decrease, then knit middle stitches on front piece, repeat picking up stitches at decrease rounds on right side (this time pick up 1 stitch at decrease followed by 1 stitch after each decrease, then knit back neck stitches. You'll have a total of 28 (32, 32, 34) stitches. Knit to desired length of turtleneck: between 8 and 12 rounds. Then bind off very loosely.

HAT

Cast on 72 (76, 80) stitches. Join and knit 60 (65, 70) rounds.

DECREASES *Knit 2 together; repeat from * to end of round. Repeat this round 2 more times. Cut yarn leaving a long tail. Thread tail in tapestry needle, then draw through remaining stitches.

Molly's Turtleneck.

SIZES
Child's small (medium, large).

YARN
Worsted-weight yarn, about 120 yards (110m).

The sample is knit with Morehouse 3-Strand; 1 skein.

NEEDLES
Size 5 or 6 (3.75 or 4mm): set of 4 or 5 double-pointed, or size to obtain correct gauge.

OTHER MATERIALS
Tapestry needle.

GAUGE
18 to 20 stitches = 4 inches (10cm) in stockinette stitch. The hat will be warmer if knit a little on the tight side.

FRINGE-BINGE
MINI MUFFLER

SIZE
Width: about 6" (15cm).
Length: 46" (117cm), not including fringe.

YARN
Sport-weight yarn, about 240 yards (219.5m).
The samples are knit with Morehouse Merino
2-Strand in (left to right, top down) Kelly,
Smokey Pearl, Sunflower, Iris, Sienna, Fuchsia,
Raspberry, Periwinkle, Natural White; 1 skein
per scarf.

NEEDLES
Size 5 or 6 (3.75 or 4mm).

OTHER MATERIALS
Decorations or embellishments for fringing
(available at fabric and craft stores); washable
fabric glue (depending on decoration) or
sewing thread and sewing needle; tapestry
needle.

GAUGE
About 24 stitches = 4 inches (10cm) over un-
stretched rib pattern (but gauge is not crucial).

Jazz up a simple ribbed scarf with show-stopping fringe. Raid your
jewelry box or button jar for gems to hang onto the ends of your
scarf, or check your local craft or fabric store for embellishments
similar to those pictured here. Keep the ornaments lightweight and
make sure they are washable, and keep small pieces that could be
choking hazards away from children under the age of four.

Cast on 34 stitches. Work pattern as follows:

PATTERN   Knit 1, *knit 2 stitches, purl 2 stitches; repeat from *
to last stitch, knit last stitch.

Repeat this row until scarf measures about 46" (117cm). Bind off
loosely.

FINISHING
Sew or glue on fringe decorations at both ends of scarf.

For fringe, use beads, bracelet charms, greeting card decorations,
and artificial floral ornaments. For fur pom-poms, thread a crocheted
or braided 5"- (13cm) long cord through a wooden bead, then cut a 2"
(5cm) circle of fur (fake or real). Coat the wrong side of fur with
fabric glue, then wrap fur around bead making sure that yarn cord
sticks out at top.

*Opposite: Fringe and embellishments created from an
assortment of decorative finds.*

BABY BLANKET WITH BOOTIES AND HAT

FOR BLANKET

SIZE

About 38" x 38" (96.5cm x 96.5cm).

YARN

Worsted-weight wool yarn in three colors, 1,200 yards (1,097m) total. About 400 yards (366m) in each color; plus about 25 yards (23m) of white or light color for border at beginning and end of blanket. The blanket will be washed and felted slightly after knitting, so choose a yarn that can be felted.

The sample is knit with Morehouse Merino 3-Strand in Smokey Pearl with Peach and Violet; 5 skeins in main color, and 2 skeins each in 2 colors, small amount of white for border.

NEEDLES

Size 4 or 5 (3.5 or 3.75mm): 29" (73.5cm) circular, or longer.

GAUGE

18 to 20 stitches and 28 rows = 4 inches (10cm) in stockinette stitch pattern.
If you knit the blanket tightly, there will be very little shrinkage widthwise in the washing and felting process; however, the length will shrink between 15% and 20%, depending on the type of yarn used.

Opposite top: Hats and booties waiting for baby to wake up from a nap.

Opposite bottom: Finishing options.

This blanket is pre-washed and slightly felted for extra warmth, making it machine washable—something a new mom will appreciate. Add the booties and hat for an additional surprise. They're so easy, you can make several sets in different colors, then tuck them away until future shower invitations arrive.

> NOTE The blanket is knit in the round as a tube, then washed and felted slightly. To avoid wavy edges at side, don't cut the blanket open until it is completely dry. Rotate it around several times during the drying process to avoid creases from forming. When completely dry, cut the blanket open between first and last stitch.

FELTING

Make a swatch using all the colors you are planning to use for the blanket. Cast on 30 stitches and knit 30 to 50 rows. Then measure swatch, or better still, make a photocopy of it on a copier—that way you'll have an image of the original to measure against, after felting the swatch. Felt the swatch in the washing machine using warm or hot water, depending on the type of yarns you are using and how much felting you want. Hot water will felt fibers more drastically and switching water temperatures from hot-water wash to cold-water rinse will produce more felting action than using warm-water wash and warm-water rinse. Note the size of your original swatch and the washing procedure used on an index card and pin the card to the felted swatch.

BLANKET

With light-color yarn for border, cast on 200 stitches. Join stitches into circle and knit 3 rounds. *Switch to color A (main color) and

knit 12 rounds, switch to color B and knit 8 rounds, back to color A and knit 12 rounds, followed by 8 rounds in color C. Cut yarn after each stripe leaving 4" (10cm) long tails. Repeat from * until blanket measures about 42" (106.5cm) from beginning. End with 12 rounds in main color. Switch to light color for border and finish blanket with 3 rounds, then bind off very loosely. Tie the yarn ends together at beginning and end of stripes—don't darn in ends, except border color at beginning and end of blanket.

FINISHING

Felt the blanket following the washing procedure marked on your index card. While washing, rearrange the blanket several times in the washing machine to avoid bunching and uneven felting. Lay blanket-tube flat to dry (don't cut it open yet) and rotate it around several times while drying to avoid creases. When the blanket is completely dry, cut it open between first and last stitch along entire length of blanket.

If you want the edges to have a more finished look, sew blanket

THE BLACK MARKER SHEEP

In the western part of America, sheep ranchers with large bands of sheep—thousands of animals—use black sheep to help them determine if the band is intact or not. Sheep get dispersed sometimes, chased or scared by predators, and they split into different groups. When this happens, the herders have to find the sheep and assemble the band again. Since they can't possibly count thousands of sheep to determine if all are present, the ranchers add black sheep: one per hundred white sheep in the band. These black sheep are called marker sheep. When it's time to round up the sheep, all the herders have to do is count the black sheep. If all are present (and can be spotted and counted easily), they know the band is complete.

We were in the mountains in Wyoming with the owner of a large band of sheep. He was telling us about the fine wool of his black marker sheep. We were very interested in finding new bloodlines because our flock of black Merino sheep was in danger of getting too inbred. We rode around in his truck until we spotted his band of sheep. Then his cowboy son got on a horse and, with the help of a sheep dog, got close enough to one of the black marker sheep to lift it up into the saddle—without getting off the horse. A circus performer couldn't have done a better job. We brought three of the black sheep back to New York. And during the first night that they spent at our farm, a coyote killed one of them.

binding at sides only or around entire blanket or finish edges with blanket stitch in a contrasting color.

BOOTIES

Cast on 34 stitches and knit 14 rows.

DECREASES Knit 20 stitches, knit 2 together (abbreviated k2tog), turn (you'll be working on middle 8 stitches), slip first stitch with yarn in front, purl 6, purl 2 together (abbreviated p2tog); turn and *slip first stitch with yarn in back, knit 6, k2 tog; turn work, slip first stitch with yarn in front, purl 6, p2tog; turn work; repeat from * three more times, then knit to end of row—you now have a total of 24 stitches.

EYELET ROW Knit first stitch, yarn over (abbreviated yo), [p2tog, yo] 3 times, p2tog, now purl 7, [yo, p2tog] 3 times, yo, k2tog. This last row created the little eyelets through which to thread the bootie ties. Now knit 20 rows for cuff, then bind off loosely. Make second bootie the same.

FINISHING

With threaded tapestry needle, sew together bottom of sole and back of bootie. With crochet hook, chain two ties each 16" (40.5cm) in length, or make 2 braids the same length to create ties (or use ribbon). Thread ties through eyelets.

HAT

Cast on 64 stitches and knit until hat measures 7½" (19cm). Work next three rows as follows: *knit 2 together; repeat from * to end of row. Cut yarn leaving a long tail. Thread tapestry needle and draw yarn through remaining stitches. Sew hat together. For accents on top of hat, crochet 5 chains (or braids) about 2" to 2½" (5 to 6.5cm) long and attach them to top of hat as follows: pull yarn ends through top of the hat at different locations, then tie the bundles together on the inside of the hat.

FOR BOOTIES AND HAT

SIZE
Newborn to 6 months.

YARN
Worsted-weight yarn, 150 yards (137m).

The samples are knit with Morehouse Merino 3-Strand; 1 skein.

NEEDLES
Size 5 or 6 (3.75 or 4mm), or size to obtain correct gauge.

OTHER MATERIALS
Size F/5 (3.75mm) crochet hook; tapestry needle; ribbon for booties (optional).

GAUGE
18 stitches = 4 inches (10cm) in garter stitch pattern.

CHAPTER FOUR

ACCESSORIES

Mittens, hats, and scarves are my favorite things to design and knit, especially mittens. Their odd shape (they look like little sacks for your hands) inspires me to come up with fun ways to decorate them. And I like to felt my mittens to make them impenetrable to cold and wetness. Several years ago, I knit a pair of man's extra-large mittens (I don't remember for whom they were meant). They looked immense and could have fit a bear's paw. So I decided to shrink them down. Whenever I did a load of laundry, I added the mittens. After several washings, they fit my hands perfectly. Now they are solid and warm, practically waterproof.

HATS WITH STRIPES

This is a good project for short strands of bulky yarn leftover from sweater and poncho projects. And if the weather forecast warns of a blizzard, you'll be finished with the topper before the first flakes fall.

SIZES
Child's small (child's medium, adult). To fit 2- to 6-year-old (7- to 12-year-old, adult medium).

YARN
Bulky yarn or worsted-weight yarn doubled in different colors, total of 120 yards (110m) bulky or twice that amount for worsted weight used doubled. Mix 'n' match by using bulky yarn for your main color and double worsted-weight yarn for the stripes.

The samples are knit with Morehouse Merino Bulky.

NEEDLES
Size 10½ or 11 (6.5 or 8mm); set of 5 double-pointed, or size to obtain correct gauge.

OTHER MATERIALS
Tapestry needle.

GAUGE
12 stitches and 21 rounds = 4 inches (10cm) in stockinette stitch.

Loosely cast on 52 (54, 58) stitches. Divide stitches evenly between 4 needles. Place marker at beginning of round and join. Knit 10 (12, 15) rounds. Switch to yarn color for stripe (don't break off main color yarn) and work stripe as follows: knit 1 round, purl 1 round. After finishing stripe, break off yarn leaving a 3" (7.5cm) tail. Instead of darning in the ends from the stripe yarn, tie the two ends together on inside of the hat using a square knot, then cut off leaving ½" (1.3cm) ends. Switch back to main color yarn and knit 5 (6, 6) rounds. Drop main color and join stripe color and add another 2-round stripe. Add as many stripes as your design calls for. Knit a total of 30 (32, 35) rounds before starting decreases.

SQUARE KNOT

CROWN SHAPING

FIRST DECREASE *Knit 5 stitches, knit 2 together; repeat from * to last 3 (5, 2) stitches, ending round with knit 3 (5, 2) stitches. Knit 1 round.

SECOND DECREASE *Knit 4 stitches, knit 2 together; repeat from * to end of round. Knit 1 round.

THIRD DECREASE	*Knit 3 stitches, knit 2 together; repeat from * to end of round. Knit 1 round.
FOURTH DECREASE	*Knit 2 stitches, knit 2 together; repeat from * to end of round. Knit 1 round.
FIFTH DECREASE	*Knit 1 stitch, knit 2 together; repeat from * to end of round. Knit another round.
SIXTH DECREASE	*Knit 2 together; repeat from * to end of round. Cut yarn leaving a 6" (15-cm) tail. Thread tapestry needle and draw yarn through remaining stitches. Weave in yarn tails.

Above: A sampling of striped hats.

Opposite: The dogs' favorite master and master's favorite hat.

DIAGONAL SCARF

Variegated yarns make most knitters' fingers itch: we love the yarns but usually hate the way they knit up. The stranding, the banding, and that bargello look are enough to keep you off the variegated-yarn bandwagon. Here is a way to knit a scarf where the difference in colors or the mismatched skeins turn into design elements instead of headaches. Knitting on the bias is another successful way of working with variegated yarns.

> NOTE This scarf is knit diagonally—from corner to corner. If you are using several different variegated colors, separate each color with a stripe in a contrasting yarn color (work 2 rows in pattern for stripe).

SIZE
About 8" (20.5cm) x 64" (162.5cm).

YARN
About 450 yards (411.5m) of variegated sport-weight yarn, odd lots, plus about 4 yards (3.7m) of light-colored sport-weight yarn. When knitting the scarf, separate the different color lots with a thin stripe of the light-colored yarn.

The samples are knit with Variegated Morehouse Merino 2-Strand, 2 skeins; and about 4 yards (3.7m) of white 2-Strand.

NEEDLES
Size 7 or 8 (4.5 or 5mm).

OTHER MATERIALS
Tapestry needle.

GAUGE
16 stitches = 4 inches (10cm) in garter stitch pattern (but gauge is not crucial).

Opposite: Mudroom décor . . . diagonally knit scarves ready for blustery days.

Cast on 2 stitches and knit first row.

INCREASE ROWS — Knit 1 stitch, increase 1 (work increases throughout scarf as follows: when knitting the first stitch, keep stitch on left-hand needle and knit into the back of the same stitch again), knit to end of row. Repeat this row until you have 50 stitches.

LENGTH — *Knit 1 stitch, increase 1, then knit across row to last 2 stitches, knit those 2 stitches together; knit next row. Repeat from * a total of 140 to 150 times (you will have knit 280 to 300 rows).

END SCARF POINT AS FOLLOWS

*Knit row to last 2 stitches, knit these 2 stitches together. Repeat from * until you have 2 stitches left. Bind off the 2 stitches.

FINISHING
Weave in loose ends. Soak scarf in warm water, squeeze out as much water as possible, and lay flat to dry, stretching scarf to final size.

DOUBLE-SIDED HAT

SIZES
Child (adult small, adult medium).

YARN
440 yards (400.5m) of sport-weight yarn in two contrasting colors, one of the colors a variegated yarn and the other a solid color (yarn color A and color B).

The samples are knit with Morehouse Merino 2-Strand in (from top) Fern Glen with Cranberry, Zest with Natural White inside, and Iris with Snake Red inside; 2 skeins—1 variegated, the other a solid color.

NEEDLES
Size 3 or 4 (3.25 or 3.5mm): 16" (40.5cm) circular; set of double-pointed needles same size, or size to obtain correct gauge. A spare 16" (40.5-cm) circular needle, same size or smaller, to use as a holding needle.

OTHER MATERIALS
Stitch marker; tapestry needle.

GAUGE
20 stitches = 4 inches (10cm) in stockinette stitch pattern.

Using variegated and solid yarns, you create two different-colored hats—one inside the other. And the extra warmth from that second hat will be welcome on cold and windy days.

With color A, cast on 92 (98, 104) stitches. Join stitches into a circle and place stitch marker for beginning of rounds. Knit in rounds until hat measures 9 (10, 10^1/$_2$)" [23 (25.5, 26.5) cm].

DECREASES   *Knit 2 stitches together; rep from * to end of round, ending up with 46 (49, 52) stitches. Put stitches on holding needle (the second circular needle).

> NOTE The cast-on edge looks like horizontal stitches. When picking up stitches, pick up 1 loop only of each horizontal stitch—the loop furthest away from you—and pull color B through the loop to create the new stitch. The other loop of each cast-on stitch will create a narrow, but neat-looking edge separating the two yarn colors.

With color B and right side of hat facing you, pick up same number of stitches as on your cast-on: 92 (98, 104) stitches around entire cast-on edge. Then knit hat with color B to same length as hat in color A. Before working next round and joining hats at the top, darn in ends at cast-on edge.

Continue with color B as follows: *knit 2 stitches together; rep from * to end of round, ending up with 46 (49, 52) stitches. Now pull color A hat inside color B hat, so that the wrong sides of both hats are facing each other. The two circular needles are now parallel to each other—one encircling the other. To join hats, switch to double-pointed needles and work next round by knitting stitches from both needles together as follows: knit first stitch on hat B together with first stitch on hat A, then second stitch on hat B together with second stitch on hat A, and so on. Use three needles from the set of double-pointed needles and divide stitches as follows: 14 (16, 16) stitches on

first needle, 16 (16, 18) stitches on second needle, and the remaining 16 (17, 18) stitches on third needle.

Bind off top of hats into three separate tips. First needle: Knit the first 7 (8, 8) stitches, then put this needle parallel to the needle holding the next 7 (8, 8) stitches. Place the needle with the not-yet-knit stitches in front and the needle with the stitches you just knit behind; using the three-needle bind off (instructions are on page 89), bind off both sets of stitches together.

Above: Worn inside out or outside in, these hats are tops for warmth.

Opposite: Marie ready for a snowball fight.

HOW DO YOU WORK
THREE-NEEDLE BIND-OFF?

Knit the first stitch on the needle closest to you together with first stitch on the needle in back, then knit second stitch on the needle closest to you together with second stitch on the needle in back, then bind off in the usual manner by lifting the first stitch over the second one. Continue this way, knitting two stitches together from the front and back needle, and binding off. Bind off last stitch by knitting the first stitch on the next needle, then binding off. Now knit to middle of the stitches on the next needle, and repeat the three-needle bind-off for second tip. Then knit to middle of the stitches on third needle and repeat the three-needle bind-off for the third and last tip.

A BEGINNER'S FANTASY

We have a scarf pattern for our bulky yarn called the Fishknit Wrap. It's a good project for beginners. It goes like this: Cast on 23 stitches and knit until you have a yard of yarn left. Now drop every other stitch off the needle and bind off the remaining stitches. Pull the dropped stitches all the way down to the beginning of the scarf. I explained this pattern to a new knitter. She thought about it for a moment, then asked, "Can I knit a second scarf with the yarn leftover from the dropped stitches?"

INDIAN CORN
SCARF AND HAT

SIZE
Width: About 8½" (21.5cm).
Length: 60" (152.5cm), not including fringe.

YARN
About 425 yards (389m) of worsted-weight yarn in corn colors. Plus about 50 yards (46m) of sport-weight or fingering-weight yarn in a light color for husk fringe. The scarf can also be made using a sport-weight yarn in two colors (golden yellow with orange brown) to achieve a corn-color combination. Work with yarn doubled (2 strands held together as one) if using sport weight.

The sample is knit with Morehouse Merino 3-Strand in Indian Corn Color, 3 skeins. Lace-weight yarn is used for fringe, 1 skein.

NEEDLE
Size 7 or 8 (4.5 or 5mm): 29" (73.5cm) circular needle (or longer). The scarf is knit length-wise, and a circular needle will accommodate the number of stitches more comfortably than straight needles.

OTHER MATERIALS
Tapestry needle.

GAUGE
14 stitches = 4 inches (10cm) in seed stitch pattern (but gauge is not crucial).

The husk-colored fringe and tassel complement the warm colors of the yarn.

An unusually colorful ear of Indian corn inspired a dye pot. The yarn turned out to be as beautiful as that ear of corn, then one thing led to another . . . and the yarn dyed in Indian corn colors became a hat and a scarf, patterned like corn kernels.

> NOTE The scarf is knit the long way.

SCARF

Cast on 211 stitches. Start pattern: *Knit 1 stitch, purl 1 stitch; repeat from * to last stitch, ending row with knit 1. Repeat this row to desired width of scarf. Bind off very loosely. The bind-off row should be as stretchy as the rest of the scarf. If you have difficulty binding off loosely, use a larger needle.

> NOTE If you work with 2 or 3 skeins of hand-painted variegated yarn, work with 2 skeins simultaneously as follows: work 2 rows in pattern with skein A, switch to skein B and work 2 rows in pattern with B. Switch to skein A and work 2 rows. Continue this way until you have used half of the skeins; break off skein A and use skein C, alternating between B and C, until you finish skein B, then start using skein A again.

By alternating skeins, the subtle differences between hand-painted variegated skeins will not be noticeable. Do not break off yarn after completing the 2 rows. Just let the yarn hang at the side of the work and continue with the next skein by pulling it up loosely to the beginning of the next row.

FRINGE

Cut strands of husk-colored lace-weight yarn 4 times the desired length of fringe plus 1" (2.5cm) for trimming. For example, if you want fringe to be 6" (15cm) long, cut strands 25" (63.5cm) long. Fold

Corn is considered a sign of prosperity by Native Americans.

each piece of fringe in half and in half again. Using a crochet hook or a knitting needle, insert the folded middle loops through edge stitch of scarf. Pull loops through the edge stitch just far enough to be able to insert ends of fringe through loops, then pull on ends to tighten loops. Insert one double-folded fringe per 2 rows along short end of scarf. Repeat fringe at other short end of scarf. Trim fringe to even lengths. Weave in loose yarn tails.

HAT

With circular needle, cast on 62 (66) stitches using yarn doubled. Join stitches into a circle, placing stitch marker for beginning of rounds.

> NOTE If you are knitting the hat using a sport-weight yarn, triple the yarn for cast-on and first 3 rounds.

Work next 3 rounds with yarn doubled as follows: purl 1 round, knit 1 round, and purl 1 round. Then break off one strand and continue hat using single yarn. Work next round as follows: *knit 2, increase 1 (increase by picking up yarn between stitches—if possible, pick up only one of the strands of yarn—then knit into back of loop to create a twisted stitch); repeat from * to end of round—93 (99) stitches.
Start seed stitch pattern:

ROUND 1   *Knit 1, purl 1; repeat from * to end of round, ending round with knit 1.

ROUND 2   *Purl 1, knit 1; repeat from * to end of round, ending with purl 1.

Repeat these 2 rounds until hat measures 7 (8)" [18 (20.5) cm] from cast-on edge.

DECREASES   Switch to double-pointed needles, if you are using circular needles. *Knit 2 together; repeat from * to end of round, knit last stitch together with first stitch on next round. Repeat this last round one more time. Use yarn doubled again, knit 1 round, then bind off on next round. There will be a hole at the top of the hat. Doubling the yarn for the last round and the bind-off serves as reinforcement to insert fringe around entire bind-off edge for tassel.

SIZES:
Child (Adult).

YARN
About 200 yards (183m) [less for child's size] of worsted-weight yarn in corn colors, plus about 20 yards (19m) of sport-weight or fingering-weight yarn in a light color for husk tassel (or use sport-weight yarn in two colors to achieve a corn-color combination and work hat using yarn doubled).

The sample is knit with Morehouse Merino 3-Strand in Prosperity Corn Color, 2 skeins. Lace-weight yarn is used for fringe, 1 skein.

NEEDLES
Size 5 or 6 (3.75 or 4mm): 16" (40.5cm) circular needle; set of double-pointed needles same size, or size to obtain correct gauge. You can also work entire hat using double-pointed needles.

OTHER MATERIALS
Stitch marker; tapestry needle.

GAUGE
20 stitches = 4 inches (10cm) in seed stitch pattern.

TASSEL

With husk-colored lace-weight yarn, cut strands 25" (63.5cm) long. Fold each strand in half and then in half again so strand measures about 6" (15cm). Using a crochet hook or a knitting needle, insert the middle loop of the strand through a bind-off stitch. Pull loop through just far enough to be able to insert ends through loop, then pull on ends to tighten loop around bind-off edge. Insert 1 fringe per stitch of bind-off edge. Trim ends evenly, then tie knot in bundle (see hat on page 91).

Enjoying the last bites of grass before winter sets in.

MOLAS MITTENS

SIZES
Woman's small (medium, large).

YARN
200 yards (183m) of worsted-weight yarn per pair.

The samples are knit with Morehouse Merino 3-Strand (2 skeins per pair).

NEEDLES
Size 4, 5, or 6 (3.5, 3.75 or 4mm); set of double-pointed, or size to obtain correct gauge.

GAUGE
20 stitches = 4 inches (10cm) in stockinette stitch pattern. Decorating the mittens will be easier if they are knit tightly.

OTHER MATERIALS
Stitch markers; stitch holder; tapestry needle. Small pieces of felt; sewing thread to match felt; sharp embroidery or sewing needle; yarns for embroidery and stitching designs (any type of color-fast yarn will do).

ABOUT MOLAS
Molas are brightly colored pieces of fabric decorated with appliqué and stitchings made by the Kuna Indian tribe on Las Blas Islands (a group of small coral islands off the coast of Panama in Central America). Traditionally used on women's blouses, molas today are highly prized by collectors around the world. The colorful decorations have inspired artists for many decades—from school children to professional textile and graphic designers.

Mittens make great gifts; these Molas-inspired designs will let you personalize each pair. Decorate them with images of a favorite pet or retell a story or an event—start with the left-hand mitten and continue the story on the right-hand one. The pair does not have to match. Stitch the pet on one mitten, and the pet's toys or activities on the other. Primary or bright colors are a must, and stitches don't have to be perfect. Don't worry if your design skills are not up to snuff. Molas are designed from the heart—not on a drawing board.

MITTENS

Cast on 36 (38, 40) stitches. Divide stitches evenly between 3 needles. Join stitches into a circle and place marker at beginning of round. Knit 18 to 24 rounds, or to desired length of cuff.

THUMB GUSSET

INCREASE ROUNDS Knit 1, place first marker, increase 1 (increase by picking up yarn between stitches and knitting into back of loop, so knit stitch appears to be twisted), knit 1, increase 1, place second marker, knit to end of round. Knit 2 rounds. Repeat these last 3 rounds a total of six times—increasing in first round after first and before second marker, then working 2 knit rounds—until you have 13 stitches between markers. End thumb gusset with knit 2 rounds.
NEXT ROUND Knit first stitch, place next 13 stitches on stitch holder (paper clip will also work), knit to end of round (pull yarn tight after that first stitch to avoid gap).
Knit 22 (25, 28) rounds (or length to cover little finger).

TOP SHAPING

DECREASE ROUND 1 *Knit 4 stitches, knit 2 together; repeat from * to end of round, knit stitches leftover (if any) at end of round. Knit 4 rounds.

Buffy under rain cloud thinking
sunny thoughts

Thumb-biting snake
under desert sun

Sheep with green eartags
leapfrogging in full moon

Purple heart reflected in water

Mole high-rise

Chickens whistling "Dixie."

DECREASE ROUND 2 *Knit 3 stitches, knit 2 together; repeat from * to end of round. Knit 3 rounds.

DECREASE ROUND 3 *Knit 2 stitches, knit 2 together; repeat from * to end of round. Knit 2 rounds.

DECREASE ROUND 4 *Knit 1 stitch, knit 2 together; repeat from * to end of round.

DECREASE ROUND 5 *Knit 2 together; repeat from * to end of round. Draw yarn through remaining stitches. Weave in yarn end, using tapestry needle.

THUMB

Place 13 stitches on 3 needles and pick up 3 (4, 4) stitches between first and last stitch—total of 16 (17, 17) stitches. Knit 17 (18, 20) rounds.

DECREASES *Knit 2 together; repeat from * to end of round. Draw yarn through remaining stitches. Weave in yarn end, using tapestry needle.

MOLAS APPLIQUÉ

The felt pieces are not only decorative, but also add an insulating layer of warmth to the mittens. Add decorations to the back side of mittens only—since there is no left- or right-hand to these mittens, put the pair in front of you, thumbs facing each other, and mark the sides facing you with a piece of yarn. Use mittens illustrated here as guidelines only. Use your own imagination and decorate your pair of mittens with a rendition of your favorite animal, plant, or object.
 The stylized depictions of animals and shapes are easy to create. Imperfections and variations will add a personal touch to your mittens. Cut felt into shapes, stripes, or squares, then sew the pieces onto the backside of the mitten. Insert a piece of hand-shaped cardboard into mitten while working on it, to avoid accidentally sewing the mitten together while applying the felt decorations or embroidering. Add stitching and embroidery as needed for your design. Use simple embroidery stitches: running stitch, back stitch, chain stitch, or satin stitch. Don't forget to give your pair of Molas Mittens a name!

MOLAS STITCHING

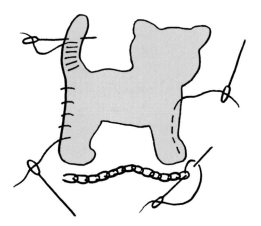

My mother knitting away on our porch.

BOJANGLES SCARF WITH HAT

My ninety-two-year-old mother contributed this design. Having lived through shortages during wars, she treasures and saves every ball of yarn and sooner or later finds a use for it. She is also very practical. Using lots of colors in a project means having to darn in lots of ends, but my mother found a way of turning this nuisance into a design element. She is creative, and at her age has long ago overcome the trappings of rigid knitting techniques. So, go ahead, pull a few colors out of your yarn stash, and don't worry about combining different weights—they add texture to the scarf.

FOR SCARF

SIZE
About 8½" (21.5cm) wide and whatever length you want to make it. Scarves can be as short as 40" (101.5cm) and as long as 80" (203cm) or longer—your choice!

YARN
For a 70" (178cm) scarf you'll need about 450 yards (411.5m) of worsted-weight yarn in lots of different colors.

The sample is knit with Morehouse Merino 3-Strand.

NEEDLES
Size 7, 8, or 9 (5.5mm).

GAUGE
About 16 stitches = 4 inches (10cm) in garter stitch pattern (but gauge is not crucial).

SCARF

Cast on 33 stitches. Knit a garter stitch stripe about 2" (5cm) wide. Change yarn color as follows: Knit 11 stitches with old color, add new yarn color (leave a tail 1" [2.5cm] or longer at beginning), and knit the next 11 stitches with both yarns; break off old color (leaving a tail about 1" [2.5cm] or longer) and continue with new color until you are ready to switch yarn colors again. Then repeat procedure for switching yarn: knit 11 stitches with old yarn, knit 11 stitches with both yarns, break off old yarn and continue with new color. Trim yarn beginnings and ends to length you like.

HAT

Cast on 80 (86) stitches. Divide stitches evenly between 4 needles. Join stitches into a circle, placing marker at beginning of round. Work in rounds as follows: purl 1 round, knit 1 round. Repeat these 2 rounds until border measures 2½ (3)" [6.5 (7.5) cm]. Knit 1 round. Knit next round and decrease 4 stitches evenly—76 (82) stitches left. **ADULT SIZE ONLY:** Knit 7 rounds.

NEXT ROUND *Knit 8 stitches, knit 2 stitches together; repeat from * to last 2 stitches, ending round with knit 2 (all subsequent decrease rounds on adult size will end with knit 2 stitches).

BOTH SIZES: Knit 7 rounds.

DECREASE ROUND 1 *Knit 7 stitches, knit 2 stitches together; repeat from * to end of round (on child's size ending this and the next four decrease rounds with knit 4).
Knit 6 rounds.

DECREASE ROUND 2 *Knit 6 stitches, knit 2 stitches together; repeat from * to end of round. Knit 5 rounds.

DECREASE ROUND 3 *Knit 5 stitches, knit 2 together; repeat from * to end of round. Knit 4 rounds.

DECREASE ROUND 4 *Knit 4 stitches, knit 2 together; repeat from * to end of round. Knit 3 rounds.

FOR HAT

SIZE
Child 8 to 12 years (adult).

YARN
145 yards (133m) of worsted-weight yarn, small amounts of different yarn colors for pom-pom.

Sample is knit with Morehouse Merino 3-Strand; 1 skein, and leftover yarn from scarf for pom-pom.

NEEDLES
Size 5 or 6 (3.75 or 4 mm); set of 5 double-pointed, or size to obtain gauge.

OTHER MATERIALS
Stitch marker, tapestry needle.

GAUGE
18 stitches = 4 inches (10cm) in garter stitch pattern.

Look, Ma: No darning in! These simple scarves are a great way to use old scraps of yarn. This set was designed by my mother.

DECREASE ROUND 5 *Knit 3 stitches, knit 2 together; repeat from * to end of round. Knit 2 rounds.

DECREASE ROUND 6 *Knit 2 stitches, knit 2 together; repeat from * to end of round. Knit 1 round.

DECREASE ROUND 7 *Knit 1, knit 2 together; repeat from * to end of round.

DECREASE ROUND 8 *Knit 2 together; repeat from * to end of round.

Cut yarn leaving a 6" tail. Thread tail into tapestry needle, then draw yarn through remaining stitches.

Add pom-poms (see next page).

Albrecht having a chat with Sage.

HOW TO MAKE A POM-POM

Cut out a donut-shaped form from plastic coffee can lids. It will be sturdier than cardboard, and you'll be able to reuse it. For a 2" (5cm) pom-pom, cut out two discs about 2 1/2" (6.5cm) in diameter (trace the bottom of a glass on the plastic coffee can lid), then cut out a hole in the middle—about 3/4" (2cm) in diameter. Now cut out a sliver (see illustration) to make wrapping easier. Put the two discs together and start wrapping yarn around the pom-pom donut. If you are using more than one color, break off the first color leaving a short tail, and continue wrapping with a new yarn color. For a full pom-pom, wrap until the small hole in the middle is completely filled.

Cut the wraps open around the outer edge of the form (between the two discs) with a pair of sharp-pointed scissors. Now insert a piece of string (I use strong cotton) between the discs and tie the wraps together. Peel away the plastic discs. Trim the pom-pom. Crochet or braid a cord 3 to 5" (7.5 to 12.5cm) long leaving a tail about 6" (15cm) long at both ends. Attach one end to pom-pom (thread yarn tail through a sharp needle, and insert needle with yarn through the center of pom-pom—pull needle out at opposite side, re-insert through center again, then tie yarn tail to cord) and attach the other end to the tip of the hat.

My husband, Albrecht, creates interesting pom-poms: he makes a really full and firm one, then trims it by sculpting it into a ram's head.

MATERIALS NEEDED

Leftover yarn (short strands work fine).

2 plastic lids from coffee cans (or 1 lid from a large can).

Piece of strong cotton or yarn, 6" to 8" (15 to 20.5cm) long.

Scissors with sharp points.

Yarn needle with sharp point.

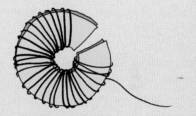

BERET

This is a French-style beret—snug fitting and chic—and the variegated yarn puts a new spin on it.

> NOTE If you are winding a skein of yarn into a ball, wind about 8 yards into a separate ball so that the first 4 rounds can be knit with yarn doubled. The border can be worked one of two ways: seed stitch or stockinette stitch.

SIZE
Adult, one size.

YARN
Variegated sport-weight yarn, 200 yards (choose a yarn that can be felted slightly).

Sample is knit with Variegated Morehouse Merino 2-Strand in Grape Juice (1 skein).

NEEDLES
Circular needle 3 or 4: 16" (40.5 cm); set of double-pointed needles same size, or size to obtain correct gauge.

OTHER MATERIALS
Stitch marker; tapestry needle.

GAUGE
22 stitches and 32 rounds = 4 inches (10cm) over stockinette stitch pattern.

Above: Marie heading out into the rain under her special umbrella from the Humane Society.

HAT

Using yarn doubled, with circular needle cast on 65 stitches. Join and place marker for beginning of rounds. If you choose seed stitch, work 4 rounds in seed stitch pattern as follows: round 1 *knit 1, purl 1, repeat from * to end of round, ending with knit 1; round 2 *purl 1, knit 1, repeat from * to end of round, ending with purl 1. Or you can work border in stockinette stitch: knit 4 rounds. If you choose stockinette stitch version, the edge will curl slightly looking like a band around the beret. The gauge on the border will be different (5 stitches per inch), because you are working with yarn doubled. Make sure border is worked tight—so it will remain firm even after years of wear. Continue with yarn single.

FIRST INCREASE ROUND   Knit 5, * increase 1, knit 1; repeat from * to end of round ending with increase 1 (you now have a total of 126 stitches). Knit 1 round.

SECOND INCREASE ROUND   Knit 6, *increase 1, knit 30; repeat from * to end of round—total of 130 stitches. Knit 45 rounds for a snug fit or 55 rounds for a floppier version.

CROWN SHAPING

FIRST DECREASE   *Knit 11 stitches, knit 2 together; repeat from * to end of round. Knit 1 round.

SECOND DECREASE	*Knit 10 stitches, knit 2 together* repeat from * to end of round. Knit 1 round.
THIRD DECREASE	*Knit 9 stitches, knit 2 together* repeat from * to end of round. Knit 1 round.
FOURTH DECREASE	*Knit 8 stitches, knit 2 together* repeat from * to end of round. Knit 1 round.
FIFTH DECREASE	*Knit 7 stitches, knit 2 together* repeat from * to end of round. Knit 1 round.
SIXTH DECREASE	*Knit 6 stitches, knit 2 together* repeat from * to end of round. Knit 1 round.
SEVENTH DECREASE	*Knit 5 stitches, knit 2 together* repeat from * to end of round. Knit 1 round. Now switch to double-pointed needles.
EIGHTH DECREASE	*Knit 4 stitches, knit 2 together* repeat from * to end of round. Knit 1 round.
NINTH DECREASE	*Knit 3 stitches, knit 2 together* repeat from * to end of round. Knit 1 round.
TENTH DECREASE	*Knit 2 stitches, knit 2 together* repeat from * to end of round. Knit 1 round.
ELEVENTH DECREASE	*Knit 1 stitch, knit 2 together* repeat from * to end of round. Knit 1 round.
TWELFTH DECREASE	*Knit 2 together* repeat from * to end of round. Repeat this last round one more time. With remaining stitches knit 6 rounds (that's for the little tip). Cut yarn leaving a 6" tail. Thread tail in tapestry needle and draw yarn through remaining stitches. Weave in yarn tails.

FINISHING

For a smooth and supersoft beret, wash in warm water with mild soap. Knead hat for several minutes to start some mild felting action. Rinse in warm water. Squeeze out as much water as possible, then lay flat to dry. Shape beret like a plate, with opening in middle forming an inner circle (you will have to stretch outer edge slightly, so beret will lay flat). Let dry. For a crisp-looking edge, iron around fold. Cover beret with a damp dishtowel and iron (on wool setting) lightly around edge.

MOZART TRIO

This set is Viennese pastry without the calories. Theresa, holding the rooster, is also Viennese. The loopy construction of this pattern design makes the set less suitable for children. I call the pattern Frogman Rib—you go a stitch deeper than you would in Fisherman Rib.

SCARF

FROGMAN RIB FOR SCARF

ROW 1   Knit first stitch, *purl 1, knit 1; repeat from * to end of row.

ROW 2   Knit first stitch, *knit 1, purl 1; repeat from * to last 2 stitches, knit last 2 stitches.

ROW 3   Knit first stitch, *purl 1, knit next stitch into stitch two rows below (row 1 of pattern; see illustration); repeat from * to last 2 stitches, purl next stitch and knit last stitch in normal fashion.

ROW 4   Knit first stitch, *knit next stitch into stitch below (row 3 of pattern); purl 1; repeat from * to last 2 stitches, knit next stitch into row below, knit last stitch in normal fashion.

Repeat rows 1 through 4 for pattern.

KNIT INTO STITCH 2 ROWS BELOW

> NOTE If you are having trouble locating the stitch 2 rows below and knitting into it, it may help to have a light source in front of, instead of behind or over, you. That way you'll be able to see the stitches in crisp silhouette form and it will be easier to locate the individual stitches and rows. It also helps if you have a towel or piece of cloth on your lap that's in a contrast color to your knitting.

FOR SCARF

SIZE
9" (23cm) wide and about 70" (178cm) long.

YARN
Worsted-weight yarn, around 450 yards (411.5m). Using a loosely spun or thick-thin type worsted-weight yarn will produce a fluffier scarf and emphasize the texture better than a tightly spun, smooth yarn will.

The scarf samples are knit with Morehouse Merino 3-Strand in natural colors; 3 skeins per scarf.

NEEDLES
Size 6 or 7 (4 or 4.5mm).

OTHER MATERIALS
Tapestry needle.

GAUGE
12 stitches = 4 inches (10cm) in pattern.

Opposite: Theresa holding a rooster—whose feet became tangled up in the scarf a few minutes after this shot was taken.

Cast on 27 stitches and work in pattern to desired scarf length. Bind off loosely on row 1 of pattern.

HAT

FROGMAN RIB WORKED IN THE ROUND FOR HAT

ROUNDS 1 & 2   *Knit 1, purl 1; repeat from * to end of round.

ROUND 3   *Knit into stitch two rows below, purl 1; repeat from * to end of round.

ROUND 4   *Knit 1, purl into stitch below; repeat from * to end of round. Repeat rounds 1 through 4 for pattern.

Cast on 74 stitches. Join stitches into a circle; placing marker for beginning of round.

Work in pattern until hat measures 11" (28cm). Switch to double-pointed needles and work next round as follows:

DECREASE ROUND *Knit 2 stitches together; repeat from * to end of round. Repeat decrease round 2 more times. Cut yarn leaving 6" (15 cm) tail, thread tapestry needle and pull needle and yarn through remaining stitches to close top and secure stitches. Weave in ends.

FOR HAT

SIZE
Adult.

YARN
Worsted-weight yarn, about 250 yards (229m).
The sample is knit with Morehouse Merino 3-Strand in Natural White; 2 skeins.

NEEDLES
Size 5 or 6 (3.75 or 4mm): 16" (40.5cm) circular needle; set of double-pointed, same size or smaller, for the last 3 rounds. Adjust needle size if necessary to obtain correct gauge.

OTHER MATERIALS
Stitch marker; tapestry needle.

GAUGE
14 stitches = 4 inches (10cm) in pattern.

MITTENS

FROGMAN PATTERN WORKED IN THE ROUND FOR MITTENS

ROUNDS 1 & 2   Knit.

ROUND 3   *Knit into stitch two rows below, knit 1; repeat from * to end of round.

ROUND 4   *Knit 1, knit into stitch below; repeat from * to end of round. Repeat rounds 1 through 4 for pattern.

Cast on loosely 24 stitches. Divide stitches between 3 needles. Join and place stitch marker for beginning of rounds. Work in pattern until mitten measures about 4" (10cm), ending with round 4. Next round: Put the first 6 stitches on a stitch holder (paper clip will also work) then cast on 4 stitches using e-loop cast-on (see page 46) knit to end of round.

Continue in pattern (next round will be round 2 of pattern) and work in pattern until mitten measures 9" (23cm), or until the tip of your fingers are covered. Work next 2 rounds as follows: *knit 2 stitches together, repeat from * to end of round. Cut yarn leaving 6" (10cm) tail, thread tapestry needle and draw needle through remaining stitches to close top and secure stitches. Weave in ends.

THUMB

Put the 6 stitches on 2 needles (3 stitches on each), pick up 6 stitches along e-loop cast-on. Work in pattern until thumb is covered—2¾" (7cm) to 3" (7.5cm) then work next round as follows: *knit 2 stitches together, repeat from * to end of round. Cut yarn leaving 6" (10cm) tail, thread tapestry needle, and draw needle through remaining stitches to close top and secure stitches. Weave in ends.

FOR MITTENS

SIZE
Woman's medium.

YARN
Worsted-weight, 250 yards (229m).
The sample (on p. 104) is knit with Morehouse Merino 3-Strand in Natural White; 1 skein.

NEEDLES
Size 5 or 6 (3.75mm or 4mm): set of double-pointed needles. It's impossible to knit tight with this pattern, but if you tend to knit loosely, use size 4 (3.5mm) needles.

OTHER MATERIALS
Stitch markers; stitch holder; tapestry needle.

GAUGE
12 stitches = 4 inches (10cm) in pattern

Mmm—accessories! Great warmth, soft texture, and no calories in this Mozart treat.

CHAPTER FIVE

SWEATERS

Sweaters are big knitting projects that often lead to broken promises, guilty feelings, and pieces and parts waiting for assembly. My sweaters are easy and quick. Knit in the round with the sleeves knit right onto them, they require little or no finishing. Classic and stylish, they will still be favorites several winters from now.

The designs are inspired by the beauty and softness of our merino wool—and by pure necessity to keep warm and comfortable on frigid January nights in the lambing barn. Just like a favorite teddy bear, these sweaters are to be loved and worn— season after season.

ALBRECHT'S SWEATER

My husband likes his sweaters plain. When I showed him the swatch with the purl rows, he called them tire tracks and chose the stockinette stitch version instead. For him, a sweater means two things: warmth and comfort. But if you prefer, add purl rounds as stripes.

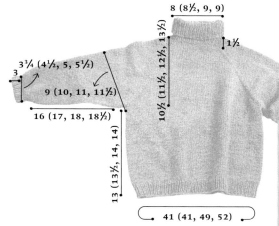

8 (8½, 9, 9)

1½

3¾ (4½, 5, 5½)

3

9 (10, 11, 11½)

16 (17, 18, 18½)

10½ (11½, 12½, 13½)

13 (13½, 14, 14)

41 (41, 49, 52)

NOTE The sweater is knit entirely in one piece from the neck down, and before separating the sleeves from the body of the sweater, you'll have between 270 and 344 stitches on the needle, depending on the size of sweater.

If stockinette stitch is too plain for you, choose a pattern for the body of the sweater (see swatch on page 112) and work in your choice of pattern. Make sure the gauge is the same. Work the pattern throughout the sweater, including the sleeves.

SIZES
Adult small (medium, large, x-large).
To fit sizes 38 (42, 46, 50)" [96.5 (106.5, 117, 127) cm].

YARN
Sport-weight yarn used doubled (in two colors) for a heather effect. 1,000 to 1,300 yards (914.5 to 1,189 m) in each color.

The sample is knit with Morehouse Merino Featherlight in Habitat; 8 (9, 10, 11 skeins).

NEEDLES
Size 8 (5mm): 16" (40.5cm), three 29" (73.5cm) circular needles (or longer); set of 4 or 5 double-pointed same size, for lower sleeve (size to obtain gauge).

OTHER MATERIALS
Tapestry needle; 4 stitch markers.

GAUGE
14 stitches and 24 rounds = 4 inches (10cm) in stockinette stitch.

Opposite: Albrecht with his team.

COLLAR

With the 16" (40.5cm) circular needle, cast on 58 (60, 62, 64) stitches. Place marker to indicate beginning of rounds and join stitches into circle. Work in rounds of knit 1, purl 1 rib to desired length of mock turtle or turtleneck collar (about 15 rounds for a mock turtle and 35 to 40 rounds for a full turtleneck collar).

RAGLAN

Work next round as follows: increase 1 stitch (increase by picking up yarn between stitches with left-hand needle and knitting into the back of the loop—creating a twisted stitch; work all increases throughout sweater this way), knit 10 (10, 10, 11) stitches, place marker, increase 1 stitch, knit 19 (20, 21, 21) stitches, place second marker, increase 1 stitch, knit 10 (10, 10, 11) stitches, place third marker, increase 1 stitch, and knit remaining 19 (20, 21, 21) stitches. *Knit 1 round. Knit next round as follows: knit first stitch, increase 1 stitch, knit to first marker, increase 1 stitch before marker, slip marker, knit 1 stitch, increase 1 stitch, knit to second marker, increase 1 stitch before marker, slip marker, knit 1 stitch, increase 1 stitch, then knit to third

Albrecht calls this rib design "tire tracks." Worked as follows: knit 4 rounds, * purl 1 round, knit 1 round; repeat from * total of 3 times.

marker, increase 1 stitch before marker, slip marker, knit 1 stitch, then increase 1 stitch, knit to fourth marker, increase 1 stitch before marker, slip marker. Repeat from * until you have 63 (69, 75, 81) stitches to first marker, and 72 (79, 86, 91) stitches between first and second marker, and again 63 (69, 75, 81) stitches to third marker, and 72 (79, 86, 91) stitches to fourth marker—a total of 270 (296, 322, 344) stitches on needle(s). Knit one round. If stitches become too crowded for one needle, divide them evenly between two circular needles and use the third one to knit with.

BODY

Now separate sleeves from body of sweater as follows: knit the first stitch, then transfer 62 (68, 74, 80) stitches onto the 16" (40.5cm) circular needle (don't knit them, just slide them onto the needle), then knit the stitches to the next marker—pull the yarn tight to avoid a gap where you transferred stitches for sleeve, knit 1 additional stitch (that's the stitch that separated the raglan increases); then transfer the next 62 (68, 74, 80) stitches onto a circular holding needle for the second sleeve, and knit the remaining stitches—again pull yarn tight to avoid a gap. There are now 146 (160, 174, 184) stitches on the working needle for the body. Continue working on body to desired length of sweater—about 13 (13½, 14, 14)" [33 (34.5, 35.5, 35.5) cm], before 2" (5cm) ribbed border begins.

RIBBED BORDER *Knit 8 stitches, knit 2 stitches together; rep from * to end of round (knit any remaining stitches at end of round). Now work 12 rounds in knit 1 purl 1 rib, then bind off loosely in rib.

SLEEVES

Start sleeve on 16" (40.5cm) circular needle. The sleeves are knit in the round. Pick up 1 stitch at beginning of round, knit to end of round and pick up 1 more stitch. Place marker at beginning of round. *Knit 4 rounds. Work next round as follows: knit 2 stitches together, knit round to last 2 stitches, and knit these 2 stitches together. Repeat from * to desired sleeve length or 16 (17, 18, 18½)"—allowing for a 3"- (7.5cm) long cuff. When the sleeve circumference is too narrow for the circular needle, switch to double-pointed needles.

CUFF Work 3" in knit 1 purl 1 rib. Bind off loosely. Weave in ends.

THE DOGS OF MOREHOUSE FARM

We have three kinds of dogs: herding dogs, guard dogs, and one pet dog. The herding dogs make life easier for a shepherd. Instead of us rounding up the sheep, the dogs will do the job for us. There are many kinds of herding dogs, and they each have unique strengths.

Sage is a Border collie, a well-known breed of herding dog. She works by eyeing the sheep, slowly and calmly walking (almost creeping) up to them, then staring at them, she will get them to move in whatever direction we indicate to her. Sage is a very polite dog; she reminds me of a cartoon I once saw of a dog tapping a sheep on the shoulder, saying, "Pardon, Miss—please move." (Sage, pictured at top, died while this book was in production. Farewell, sweet animal!)

Our black dog, Jet, is a breed of herding dog called hunt-away, he moves the sheep more aggressively by charging at them and barking. But that's the only way to get a bunch of horned Merino rams to move.

Our three guard dogs—two Great Pyrenees and one Maremma—keep the sheep safe from predators and from free-roaming dogs. Jasper, the Maremma, is the star of our sheep guard. Maremmas are an Italian breed of dogs used in the Alps to guard sheep against wolves. They are domesticated, but they prefer living with sheep to living with people. Jasper is in charge of the neighbor's farm where our ewe flock lives. He patrols close to 300 acres with extraordinary alertness and dedication. This dog is worth his weight in gold. May he live forever! Our two Great Pyrenees are a little lazy— they prefer hanging out with people to guarding sheep.

And then there is our pet dog. When our old pet dog died a few years back, I went to the local animal shelter in search of a replacement. I had no particular style, type, or breed in mind: I simply wanted a "sensible" dog. There were dozens of dogs at the shelter barking wildly and racing around their enclosures, except for one—who was obviously old—sitting in a corner minding her own business. That's the one I chose—very much to the relief of the shelter's staff. She was considered "unadoptable" and had spent the last two years waiting for a home. She turned out to be the best choice for our farm. Chickens, geese, sheep, cats, and other dogs—this dog likes them all. We named her Keepsie, short for the town of Poughkeepsie where she was found.

(Top to bottom) Sage, the Border collie; Bari, one of the Great Pyrenees; Jet, the moving ram dog; Keepsie—no beauty, but a sensible dog; Jasper, the star.

JEFF'S VEST

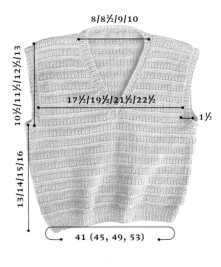

8/8½/9/10

10½/11½/12½/13

17½/19½/21½/22½

1½

13/14/15/16

41 (45, 49, 53)

Knit/purl patterns easily turn plain and ordinary garments into striking, textured knits. Most men seem to gravitate towards this low-key, but classic look, or is it only the men on this farm?

STITCH PATTERN
(WORKED IN THE ROUND FOR BODY)

ROUNDS 1 TO 4	Knit.
ROUND 5	Purl.
ROUND 6	Knit.
ROUNDS 7 TO 10	*Knit 1 stitch, purl 1 stitch; repeat from * to end of round.

STITCH PATTERN (WORKED BACK AND FORTH FOR FRONT AND BACK AFTER ARMHOLE DIVISION)

ROWS 1 & 3	Knit.
ROWS 2 & 4	Purl.
ROWS 5 & 6	Purl.
ROWS 7 & 9	*Knit 1 stitch, purl 1 stitch; repeat from * across row, ending with knit 1.
ROWS 8 &10	Knit first stitch, *knit 1 stitch, purl 1 stitch*; repeat from * across row.

NOTE This vest is knit in the round to armholes.

BODY

With smaller needle, cast on 186 (204, 222, 240) stitches. Place marker to indicate beginning of round and join. Work 12 to 16 rounds in rib pattern as follows: *knit 1 stitch, purl 1 stitch*; rep from * to end of round. Switch to larger needle. Knit next round and increase 20 (22, 24, 26) stitches evenly—for a total number of stitches of 206 (226, 246, 266). Start pattern and work until vest or sweater measures about 13 (14, 15, 16)" [33 (35.5, 38, 40.5) cm] or desired length to armhole (measured from cast-on edge), ending with round 1 of pattern.

SIZES
Adult small (medium, large, x-large).
To fit sizes 38 (42, 46, 50)" [96.5 (106.5, 117, 127) cm].

YARN
Worsted-weight yarn, 980 to 1,250 yards (896 to 1,143m).

The sample is knit with Morehouse Merino 3-strand in Cranberry (7 to 9 skeins).

NEEDLES
Size 4 or 5 (3.5 or 3.75mm): 24" (61cm) circular (or longer) for rib border (size to obtain gauge).
Size 5 or 6 (3.75 or 4mm): 24" (61cm) circular (or longer) for body; 16" (40.5cm) circular for armhole and neckline borders (size to obtain gauge). Spare circular needles in smaller sizes to use as stitch holders.

OTHER MATERIALS
Stitch marker, tapestry needle.

GAUGE
20 stitches and 32 rows = 4 inches (10cm) in stockinette stitch pattern.

Opposite: Jeff shearing a Merino ram. Shearing is strenuous work. To keep his back from getting stiff, Jeff keeps warm with his special merino vest.

DIVIDE FOR ARMHOLES

Work next round (round 2 of pattern) as follows: knit 99 (109, 117, 127) stitches, bind off the next 8 (8, 12, 12) stitches; knit the next 95 (105, 111, 121) stitches and place them on spare needle for front, then bind off the last 4 (4, 6, 6) stitches on round and the first 4 (4, 6, 6) stitches on next round.

BACK

Continue working on the first half of stitches for back piece. Adjust pattern to working back and forth (beginning with row 3—a knit row). Bind off 2 stitches at the beginning of the next 2 (2, 2, 4) rows; then bind off 1 stitch at the beginning of the next 4 rows. Continue in pattern until piece measures 10½ (11½, 12½, 13)" [26.5 (29, 31.5, 33) cm] from armhole division. Put stitches on spare needle (use smaller circular needle from border).

Who's next?

FRONT

Slip stitches from holding needle to working needle. Attach yarn at right side of piece and work row 3 of pattern. Bind off 2 stitches at the beginning of the next 2 (2, 2, 4) rows; then bind off 1 stitch at the beginning of the next 4 rows. You have a total of 87 (97, 103, 109) stitches now. Work 43 (48, 51, 54) stitches. The next stitch (middle stitch) will be the beginning of your V-neck. Thread a piece of different colored yarn through the stitch to mark it, and to prevent it from running (a paper clip works well too), then drop the stitch from needle. Put remaining 43 (48, 51, 54) stitches on spare needle for right front. Work back to beginning of row to armhole edge. Continue working on left front.

V-NECK DECREASES Work in pattern to last 2 stitches at neck edge, knit last 2 stitches together. Turn and work in pattern back to beginning of row. Continue working in pattern and every fourth row knit 2 stitches together at neck edge. Work to same length as back piece. Now bind off shoulders together using three-needle bind-off. Put front and back pieces parallel to each other, wrong sides facing out, and bind off together (see Three-Needle Bind-Off on page 89). Continue until all stitches on left front are bound off. Repeat for right front. The remaining stitches are those designated for the back neck.

NECK BAND

With 16" (40.5cm) circular needle and right side facing, pick up stitches starting at left shoulder as follows: pick up 1 stitch per 2 rows, then pick up middle stitch at bottom of V-neck (with colored yarn tied to it; keep yarn tied to stitch to mark it) and continue picking up 1 stitch per 2 rows on right side of V-neck, then knit the stitches along the back neck. Place marker to indicate beginning of rounds and join. Purl first round—and at both shoulders purl 2 stitches together.

RIBBING Work next round as follows: *knit 1, purl 1; repeat from * to stitch before middle stitch, slip the next 2 stitches as if to knit (slip them simultaneously as one stitch), knit the stitch after the middle stitch, then pass the two slipped stitches over this stitch (the middle stitch will form a continuous vertical chain through the ribbed

How do you like my new look?

border). Continue in knit 1, purl 1 pattern to beginning of round. Repeat this round 3 more times. Then bind off loosely in rib—at middle stitch, work decrease as before, then bind off. Weave in ends.

ARMHOLE BANDS

With 16″ (40.5cm) circular needle, pick up stitches around armhole as follows: with right side facing, starting at armhole division, pick up 1 stitch per stitch at bind-off, 1 stitch per decrease, and 1 stitch per 2 rows at side. Place marker to indicate beginning of round and join. Purl first round and at shoulder, purl 2 stitches together. Work 4 rounds in knit 1 purl 1 rib, bind off loosely in rib on 5th round. Repeat for other armhole. Weave in ends.

NIFTY THINGS TO DO WITH TUFTS OF WOOL

First, wash the shorn wool in hot water with plenty of soap. Rinse it in hot water several times, then squeeze out as much water as possible and fluff it out to dry in an airy, open space.

- Make a felt ball for your cat to play with. Take a handful of wool, wet it, and add a drop of liquid soap. Then rub the wool between the palms of your hand until it felts into a ball.
- Knit tufts into mittens with the ends on the inside for cozy warmth. (Don't forget to add a few stitches to the mittens to allow for the additional bulk).
- Dust your furniture (dust will cling to the wool fibers).
- Line your jewelry box. Or line a bird's nest. Better still, let the birds do it themselves.
- In England, Parliament members sat on wool sacks during sessions to inspire respect for the wool trade. Please try it!
- Put a layer of wool into your hiking boots for a walk on the clouds.
- Stuff a tiny amount into a ballerina's toe shoes.
- Use it to buff your shoes to a spit-shine.
- If you store your knitting needles in a jar or a vase, put some wool at the bottom to protect the tips of the needles.

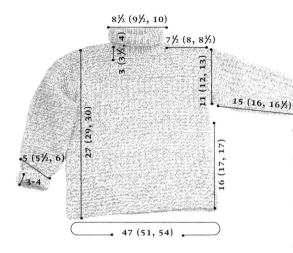

8½ (9½, 10)
7½ (8, 8½)
4 (3½, 4)
3 (3½, 4)
11 (12, 13)
15 (16, 16½)
27 (29, 30)
16 (17, 17)
5 (5½, 6)
3-4
47 (51, 54)

ERIN'S TUNIC

Which side of the tunic will be the right side? You don't have to decide until you are ready to bind off at the shoulders. As I was knitting this piece, I had planned to use the side that was facing me as the right side. But at the last moment—while doing the three-needle bind-off at the shoulders (and you have to turn the tunic wrong side out for that step)—I decided that the wrong side looked much better than the right side. So I switched and used the inside as my outside. If this sounds too confusing, knit the tunic and before binding off the shoulders, decide which side you like best.

SIZES
Oversized small-medium (medium-large, large-x-large).

To fit sizes: 38-40 (42-44, 46-48)" [96.5-101.5 (106.5-112, 117-122) cm].

YARN
Worsted-weight yarn, used doubled; 1300 to 1800 yards.

The Sample is knit with Morehouse Merino Featherlight in Woodpecker, used doubled; 10-14 skeins.

NEEDLES
Size 15 (10mm): 29" (73.5cm) circular needle (or longer); 16" (40.5cm) long for turtleneck and beginning of sleeves (the sleeves are knit in the round and are worked right onto sweater by picking up stitches around armhole opening), or size to obtain gauge; set of double-pointed, same size, for cuff and narrower part of sleeves. (You can also work the entire sleeve and neckline using double-pointed needles.) Spare circular needles in smaller size for stitch holders.

OTHER MATERIALS
Stitch marker, tapestry needle.

GAUGE:
9 stitches and 16 rounds = 4 inches (10cm).

Opposite: Erin adding our new variegated color combinations to our website.

STITCH PATTERN (WORKED IN THE ROUND FOR BODY OF TUNIC AND SLEEVES)

ROUND 1   *Knit 1 stitch, purl 1 stitch; repeat from * to end of round.

ROUND 2   Knit.

PATTERN WORKED BACK AND FORTH FOR FRONT AND BACK AFTER DIVIDING FOR ARMHOLE

ROUND 1   *Knit 1 stitch, purl 1 stitch; repeat from * to end of row, ending with knit 1.

ROUND 2   Purl.

> NOTE This tunic is knit in the round using a circular needle and is knit using yarn doubled—you'll be knitting with two skeins simultaneously.

BODY

Cast on 106 (114, 122) stitches. Place marker to indicate beginning of rounds and join. Work in pattern until tunic measures 16 (17, 17)" [40.5 (43, 43) cm] or desired length to armhole division, ending with row 2 of pattern.

DIVIDE FOR ARMHOLES

Work 53 (57, 61) stitches in pattern. Place remaining stitches on spare needle for back.

FRONT

Turn and purl back, adjusting pattern to working back and forth. Continue working back and forth until piece measures 7½ (8½ , 9)" [19 (21.5 , 23) cm]—you'll have worked about 30 (34, 36) rows, ending with row 2 of pattern.

NECK SHAPING

Work 1 row in pattern.

NEXT ROW (ROW 2 OF PATTERN) Work 23 (24, 26) stitches in pattern, bind off middle 7 (9, 9) stitches, then work remaining stitches in pattern. Continue on left side. At neck edge bind off 2 stitches 3 times. Then work 6 (6, 8) more rows even in pattern. Leave stitches on holding needle. Repeat for right side. Adjust row 1 to keep pattern consistent: with even-numbered amount of stitches, begin row with purl stitch.

BACK

Slip the stitches from the spare needle to working needle. Work back in pattern to same length as the front pieces. Then bind off shoulders together using three-needle bind-off (now is the last moment to decide which side you want to be the right side). With wrong side facing out, align needles and stitches from back and front pieces parallel to each other and bind off together (see page 89 for Three-Needle Bind-Off). Bind off both shoulders. The remaining stitches are the middle stitches on the back piece.

TURTLENECK

With 16" (40.5cm) circular needle (or double-pointed needles), pick up stitches around neckline. Start at left shoulder, with right side facing out, pick up 1 stitch per 2 rows along straight sections of neck edge (where you worked the straight rows after neck decreases) and 1 stitch per stitch along the front necks, including the bind-offs. Then add stitches from back by knitting them. Now work turtleneck in knit 1, purl 1 rib to desired length—from 6" to 8" (15 to 20.5cm). Bind off very loosely.

SLEEVES

Pick up stitches around armhole using 16" (40.5cm) circular needle. Pick up stitches as follows: beginning at underarm location and with right side facing out, pick up 1 stitch per 2 rows plus 1 additional stitch each at shoulder and at underarm location. You should end up with a total of about 48 (50, 54) stitches around entire armhole. Place marker to indicate the beginning of rounds and join. *Work 9 rounds in pattern.

DECREASE ROUND (ROUND 2 OF PATTERN) Knit 2 stitches together, knit to last 2 stitches, knit these 2 stitches together (after uneven-numbered decreases [first, third, etc.], begin row 1 of pattern with a purl stitch). Repeat from * total of 6 times. Now work in pattern to desired sleeve length (or 15, 16, 16½"), allowing for 3" (7.5 cm) cuff.

CUFF

Work next round as follows: *knit 1 stitch, knit 2 stitches together; repeat from * to end of round. If you end up with an uneven number of stitches, knit last stitch together with first stitch. Work 3" (7.5 cm) in knit 1 purl 1 rib. Bind off loosely in rib. Repeat for other sleeve.

FINISHING

Weave in yarn tails.

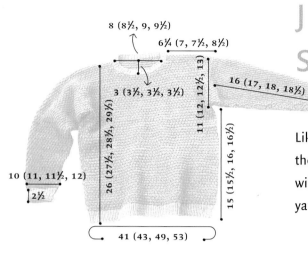

8 (8½, 9, 9½)

6¼ (7, 7½, 8½)

3 (3½, 3½, 3½)

16 (17, 18, 18½)

11 (12, 12½, 13)

26 (27½, 28½, 29½)

15 (15½, 16, 16½)

10 (11, 11½, 12)

2½

41 (43, 49, 53)

JEFF'S MOSAIC SWEATER AND SOCKS

Like small pieces of colorful glass, variegated stitches poke through the surface of this sweater. And with the variegated yarn, each stitch will be a different color. Knit socks in a complimentary variegated yarn for a nice coordinating touch.

SIZES
Adult small (medium, large, x-large).
To fit sizes 38 (42, 46, 50)" [96.5 (106.5, 117, 127) cm].

YARN
Worsted-weight yarn, 1,500 to 1,900 yards (1,371 to 1,737m), plus 150 to 200 yards (137 to 183m) in variegated color.

The sample is knit with Morehouse Merino 3-Strand in Aubergine with Fern Glen, the ribbed borders are in Cranberry; 10 to 13 skeins in solid color, 2 skeins in variegated color.

NEEDLES
Size 4 or 5 (3.5 or 3.75mm): 16" (40.5-cm) circular for neckline, sleeves (or use double-pointed needles); 24" (61cm) circular, or longer, for rib border; set of double-pointed for cuffs on sleeves.

Size 6 or 7 (4 or 4.5mm) 24" (61cm) circular, or longer, for body; 16" (40.5-cm) for sleeves; set of double-pointed for narrower part on sleeve; spare circular needles for stitch holders. Or sizes to obtain correct gauge.

OTHER MATERIALS
Tapestry needle.

GAUGE
20 stitches and 27 rows= 4 inches (10cm) in pattern stitch using larger needle.

Opposite: Jeff showing off his new sweater and one of our Merino rams.

NOTE Don't break off yarn when you switch colors, just pull the yarn up loosely on inside of sweater and cross over with yarn color you just finished working with to avoid gap between stitches. ("Crossing yarns over" means the yarn you finished with points toward the left-hand needle and the new color comes up behind and over it.)

STITCH PATTERN (WORKED IN THE ROUND FOR BODY)

ROUND 1 (MAIN COLOR) Knit.

ROUND 2 (MAIN COLOR) *Knit 1 stitch, purl 1 stitch; repeat from * to end of round.

ROUND 3 (VARIEGATED COLOR) *Slip stitch as if to purl with yarn in back, knit 1 stitch; repeat from * to end of round.

ROUND 4 (MAIN COLOR) Knit.

ROUND 5 (MAIN COLOR) *Purl 1 stitch, knit 1 stitch; repeat from * to end of round.

ROUND 6 (VARIEGATED COLOR) *Knit 1 stitch, slip next stitch as if to purl stitch with yarn in back; repeat from * to end of round.

STITCH PATTERN (WORKED BACK AND FORTH FOR FRONT AND BACK AFTER ARMHOLE DIVISION)

NOTE You'll have to use a circular needle for this straight portion, because on rows 4 and 6 the new yarn color will be at the other end of the needle.

Knit-picking geese.

ROW 1 (RIGHT SIDE, MAIN COLOR) Knit. Turn work.

ROW 2 (WRONG SIDE, MAIN COLOR) *Purl 1 stitch, knit 1 stitch; repeat from * to last stitch, ending row with purl 1 stitch. Turn work.

ROW 3 (RIGHT SIDE, VARIEGATED) Knit first stitch, *knit 1 stitch, slip next stitch as if to purl with yarn in back; repeat from * to last 2 stitches, knit these 2 stitches. Do not turn; slide stitches to other end of needle.

ROW 4 (RIGHT SIDE, MAIN COLOR) Knit. Turn work.

ROW 5 (WRONG SIDE, MAIN COLOR) *Knit 1 stitch, purl 1 stitch; repeat from * to last stitch, ending row with knit 1 stitch. Do not turn; slide stitches to other end of needle.

ROW 6 (WRONG SIDE, VARIEGATED) Knit first stitch, *slip 1 stitch as if to purl with yarn in front, purl next stitch; repeat from * to end of row. Turn work.

Repeat rows 1 through 6 for pattern.

BODY

With smaller circular needle and main color yarn or contrast yarn for ribbed borders (as in Jeff's sweater), cast on 186 (204, 222, 240) stitches. Place marker to indicate the beginning of round and join. Work 12 to 16 rounds in rib pattern as follows: *knit 1 stitch, purl 1 stitch; rep from * to end of round. Switch to larger circular needle. Knit next round, and increase 20 (22, 24, 26) stitches spaced evenly across the row for a total of 206 (226, 246, 266) stitches. Start pattern and work until body measures about 15 (15½, 16, 16½)" [38 (39, 40.5, 42) cm], from cast-on edge, or desired length to armhole, ending with round 6 of pattern.

DIVIDE FOR ARMHOLES

Work 103 (113, 123,133) stitches in pattern to middle of round. Place remaining stitches on spare needle for back.

FRONT

Turn and work back. Adjust pattern to working back and forth. Continue in pattern until front piece measures 8 (8½, 9, 9½)" [20.5 (21.5, 23, 24) cm] from armhole division, ending with row 3 or 6 of pattern. Work 1 row in pattern.

NECKLINE DECREASES Work 41 (45, 51, 55) stitches in pattern, then bind off the next 21 (23, 21, 23) stitches, and work remaining stitches in pattern. Continue on left side of front as follows: at neck edge bind off 2 stitches 5 (5, 6, 6) times, then work in pattern until armhole measures total of 11 (12, 12½, 13)" [28 (30.5, 31.5, 33) cm]. Leave stitches on spare holding needle. Repeat for right front.

BACK

Slip stitches from first spare needle to working needle. Work in pattern to same length as the two front pieces. Now bind off shoulders together using three-needle bind-off. Put front and back pieces together, wrong sides facing out, and bind off (see Three-Needle Bind-Off on page 89). The remaining stitches are for the back neck.

COLLAR

Switch to smaller circular needle (and contrast color, if used for ribbed border) and pick up stitches around neckline as follows: starting at left shoulder, right side facing out, pick up 1 stitch per 2 rows along the left side of the neck until you get to neck decreases; then pick up 1 stitch per stitch along the front neck; pick up 1 stitch per 2 rows along the right side of the neck; pick up 1 additional stitch at each shoulder and knit stitches along back neck. Place marker and join. Work 5 or 6 rounds in knit 1 purl 1 rib. In first round (and only in first round) knit (or purl, if rib pattern calls for a purl stitch) 2 stitches together at each shoulder. Bind off loosely.

SLEEVES

Pick up stitches around armhole using larger 16" (40.5cm) circular needle. Pick up stitches as follows: beginning at underarm location, right side facing out, pick up about 4 stitches per inch (approximately 2 stitches per 3 rows) and pick up 1 additional stitch each at shoulder and at underarm location—to a total of 90 (98, 104, 110) stitches. Place marker to indicate the beginning of rounds and join. Work rounds 1 to 6 of pattern. Next, work decrease round as follows: knit first 2 stitches together, knit round to last 2 stitches, knit these 2 stitches together. From here, repeat decrease round every sixth round. Adjust pattern (to account for decreases) as follows: after the first, third, fifth, etc. (uneven numbered), decreases, skip 3 rounds ahead; after even-numbered decreases (second, fourth, sixth, etc.) follow pattern as written. Work to desired sleeve length, allowing for 2½" (6.5cm) cuff—about 16 (17, 18, 18½)" [40.5 (43, 45.5, 47) cm]. Switch to larger double-pointed needles, when sleeve circumference becomes too small for 16" (40.5cm) circular needle.

CUFF Knit and decrease 4 (6, 8, 10) stitches evenly spaced around. Switch to smaller double-pointed needles (and contrast color, if used for ribbing) and work in knit 1, purl 1 rib until cuff measures 2½" (6.5cm). Bind off loosely. Repeat for other sleeve.

SOCKS

Hand-knit wool socks are a treat for your feet. And merino wool socks are a special treat. Just remember to reinforce heels and toes so the pair will last longer (fine wool is not as strong as coarser wool). Cast on 42 (44, 46, 48) stitches. Distribute stitches as follows: 10 (11, 11, 12) stitches on first needle, 11 (11, 12, 12) stitches on second and third needle, and 10 (11, 11, 12) stitches on fourth one (this arrangement makes heel shaping easier later on). Join round and work in your choice of cuff pattern to desired length to ankle.

HEEL FLAP

Join reinforcing yarn and work together with the sock yarn as one. You'll be using stitches from the first and the fourth needle and working rows back and forth. Knit 10 (11, 11, 12) stitches, turn and work on wrong side of sock back to beginning of the row as follows: Slip first stitch as if to purl with yarn in front, purl 18 (20, 20, 22) stitches (you'll be using stitches from fourth needle to complete the number of stitches required for heel), then knit one more stitch—for a total of 20 (22, 22, 24) stitches for heel. You may want to put them on one needle instead of two; put the extra needle aside for now. Turn again (right side facing you), slip first stitch as before and knit the remaining 19 (21, 21, 23) stitches on heel. Turn again, slip first stitch and purl to last stitch, knit last stitch. Repeat these 2 rows until you have a total of 20 (22, 22, 24) rows.

SIZES
Child's medium or woman's small (woman's medium/ woman's large or man's small/ man's large); for length of sock heel to toe measurement—draw footprint on paper.

YARN
From 225 to 300 yards (206–274m) of worsted weight yarn; 10 to 15 yards (9 to 14m) of nylon or other synthetic yarn to reinforce heels and toes; or knit heels and toes using yarn doubled.

The samples are knit with Morehouse Merino 3-Strand; 2 skeins per pair.

NEEDLES
Size 4 or 5 (3.5 or 3.75mm): set of 5 double-pointed needles, or size to obtain gauge.

OTHER MATERIALS
Tapesty needle.

GAUGE
22 to 24 stitches = 4 inches (2.5cm) in stockinette stitch (tightly knit socks will wear better).

TURNING HEEL

Slip first stitch, knit 13 (14, 14, 15) stitches, then knit next 2 stitches together turn; *slip first stitch as if to purl with yarn in front, purl 8 (8, 8, 10) stitches, then purl 2 together, turn; slip first stitch as if to knit this time with yarn in back, knit 8 (8, 8, 10) stitches, then knit 2 stitches together; turn; repeat from * until you have 10 (10, 10, 12) stitches left; you'll finish with row on wrong side—slip stitch, purl 8 (8, 8, 10) stitches, purl 2 together. Break off reinforcing yarn and continue with sock yarn only. Now turn— you'll be working on right side—and slip first stitch as if to purl with yarn in back, then knit 4 (4, 4, 5) stitches. With new needle

(the one you put aside when you started heel) knit the remaining 5 (5, 5, 6) stitches; then, using the same needle, pick up 11 (12, 12, 13) stitches along heel flap edge (working toward second needle). Pick up stitches as follows: 1 stitch in each slipped stitch (1 stitch per 2 rows) on heel and 1 additional stitch before stitches on second needle. Knit stitches on second and third needle. Then pick up 11 (12, 12, 13) stitches along other side of heel and—using the same needle—knit those 5 (5, 5, 6) stitches left over from the heel. You now have a total of 54 (56, 58, 62) stitches.

DECREASES *Knit 2 rounds. Next, work decrease round as follows: knit stitches on first needle to last 2 stitches, knit last 2 stitches together; knit stitches on second and third needle; on fourth needle, slip next 2 stitches one at a time as if to knit and knit them together, then knit remaining stitches. Repeat from * until you have 42 (44, 46, 48) stitches again. Next, knit until small toe is covered (use footprint as a guide or try socks on).

TOE SHAPING

Join reinforcing yarn again, and work together with sock yarn as follows:

FIRST DECREASE	*Knit 4, knit 2 together; repeat from * to end of round (on the two middle sizes, end round with knit 2— 4 stitches). Knit 4 rounds.
SECOND DECREASE	*Knit 3, knit 2 together; repeat from * to end of round (again, knit remaining stitches on middle sizes). Knit 3 rounds.
THIRD DECREASE	*Knit 2, knit 2 together; repeat from* to end of round. Knit 2 rounds.
FOURTH DECREASE	*Knit 1, knit 2 together; repeat from * to end of round. Knit 1 round.
FINAL DECREASE	*Knit 2 together; repeat from * to end of round. Cut yarn leaving 6" (15 cm) tail and thread tapestry needle. Draw needle through remaining stitches once or twice to close and secure toe. Weave in loose ends.

Opposite: An eyeful (and bowl full) of knitting material.

KIM'S JACKET

This is the perfect "when in doubt" jacket: wear it in between seasons, between afternoon and evening, between work and play. Its loose fit rates high on the comfort scale, and if you pick a neutral color, it will make few demands on your wardrobe. The unusual border around the edge will have your knitting friends guessing how you did it.

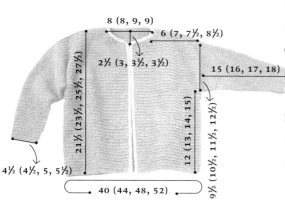

8 (8, 9, 9)
6 (7, 7½, 8½)
2½ (3, 3½, 3½)
15 (16, 17, 18)
21½ (23½, 25½, 27½)
12 (13, 14, 15)
9½ (10½, 11½, 12½)
4½ (4½, 5, 5½)
40 (44, 48, 52)

STITCH PATTERN

ROW 1	Knit.
ROW 2	*Knit 1 stitch, purl 1 stitch; repeat from * to end of row, ending row with knit 1.
ROWS 3–4	Knit.

BODY

With smaller circular needle, cast on 181 (197, 213, 233) stitches. Knit first row. Now start with row 1 of pattern (right-side row). Continue in pattern to desired length to armhole division (from 12" to 15"/ [30.5 to 38] cm).

LEFT FRONT

Work 47 (51, 55, 59) stitches in pattern; put remaining stitches on hold using spare needle. Turn and work in pattern back to beginning of row. Continue working on these 47 (51, 55, 59) stitches for left front. Work in pattern until left front measures 7 (7½, 8, 9)" [18 (19, 20.5, 23) cm] from armhole division.

START NECK DECREASES

At beginning of rows on right side bind off stitches as follows:

SMALL Bind off 6 stitches 1 time; bind off 4 stitches 1 time; bind off 2 stitches 4 times—29 stitches remain; work 10 rows even in pattern.

MEDIUM Bind off 6 stitches 1 time; bind off 4 stitches 1 time; bind off 2 stitches 4 times—33 stitches remain; work 12 rows even in pattern.

SIZES
Adult small (medium, large, x-large). Loose-fitting button-less jacket to fit sizes 36 (40, 44, 48)" [91.5 (101.5, 112, 122) cm].

YARN
Worsted-weight yarn, 1,200 to 1,800 yards (1,097 to 1,646m), plus about 7 yards (6.5m) of bulky yarn in a contrasting color for border (or use worsted-weight yarn doubled).

The sample is knit with Morehouse Merino 3-Strand in Natural Brown Heather, 9 to 12 skeins; plus about 7 yards (6.5m) of Bulky for border in Persimmon.

NEEDLES
Size 4 or 5 (3.5 or 3.75mm): 29" (73.5cm) circular, or longer; 16" (40.5cm) for sleeves; set of double-pointed needles for narrower part of sleeve. Or size to obtain gauge. Size 8 or 9 (5 or 5.5mm): 29" (73.5cm) circular, or longer, for border; spare circular needles in smaller sizes for stitch holders. Note: The jacket is knit in one piece, including the sleeves, so longer needles are useful.

OTHER MATERIALS
Stitch marker, tapestry needle.

GAUGE
18 stitches and 32 rows = 4 inches (10cm) in pattern.

Kim likes elegant cars, and she worships the sun.

LARGE Bind off 6 stitches 2 times; bind off 2 stitches 4 times—
35 stitches remain; work 14 rows even in pattern.

X-LARGE Bind off 6 stitches 2 times; bind off 2 stitches 4 times—
39 stitches remain, work 14 rows even in pattern.

FOR ALL SIZES Put stitches on spare holding needle.

RIGHT FRONT

Slip 47 (51,55, 59) stitches at right end of first spare needle to working
needle and work in same manner as left front, reversing neck shaping.

BACK

Slip remaining 87 (95, 103, 115) stitches from spare needle to
working needle and work in pattern to same length as the two fronts.
Work last row as follows: work 29 (33, 35, 39) stitches in pattern,
bind off the next 29 (29, 33, 37) stitches loosely; work remaining 29
(33, 35, 39) stitches in pattern. Now bind off shoulders together using
three-needle bind-off (see Three-Needle Bind-Off on page 89).

Royalty residing at Morehouse Farm.

SLEEVES

With 16" (40.5cm) circular needle, pick up stitches around armhole opening as follows: Start at underarm location, right side facing out, and pick up 1 stitch per 2 rows along armhole. Pick up 1 additional stitch at shoulder and at underarm location. Place marker to indicate beginning of round and join. Work 5 rounds in pattern. Decrease on next round as follows: Knit the first 2 stitches together, knit round to last 2 stitches, knit these 2 stitches together. *Work 5 rounds in pattern, repeat decrease round on 6th round (adjust pattern on round 2—after first, third, fifth etc. decrease round, begin round with purl stitch). Repeat from * to desired sleeve length, approximately 15" to 18" (40.5 to 45.5cm), or until you have 44 stitches left. Then continue in pattern to desired length. Switch to double-pointed needles when sleeve gets too narrow for circular needle. Bind off loosely. Repeat for other sleeve.

FRONT AND NECK BORDER

With worsted-weight yarn and smaller long circular needle, right side facing out, pick up stitches. Start at bottom of right front and pick up 1 stitch per 2 rows along front edge; pick up 1 additional stitch at end of right front; pick up 1 stitch per stitch along bound-off section of neck, then pick up 1 stitch per 2 rows on straight part after neckline decreases; pick up 1 stitch per stitch along back neck and repeat pick-up sequence on left front.

NEXT ROW (WRONG SIDE) Switch to larger needle and bulky yarn and knit row (you'll be working on wrong side).

BIND-OFF ROW Switch back to smaller needle and worsted-weight yarn—now at the other end of the needle. Slide stitches to end of row and with worsted-weight yarn and smaller needle, knit row and bind off loosely at the same time.

Detail of the border on Kim's Jacket.

DEBBIE'S SWEATER

An update on the sweater girl look. Cowl neck, short waist, and knit with soft merino wool; hand-knit sweaters are cropping up everywhere—in the dining room, classroom, boardroom, and even the ballroom.

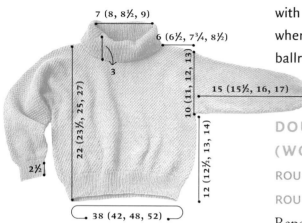

7 (8, 8½, 9)
6 (6½, 7¾, 8½)
3
15 (15½, 16, 17)
10 (11, 12, 13)
22 (23½, 25, 27)
12 (12½, 13, 14)
2½
38 (42, 48, 52)

DOUBLE SEED STITCH PATTERN (WORKED IN THE ROUND)

ROUNDS 1 & 2 *Knit 1, purl 1; repeat from * to end of round.

ROUNDS 3 & 4 *Purl 1, knit 1; repeat from * to end of round.

Repeat rounds 1 through 4 for pattern.

DOUBLE SEED STITCH PATTERN (WORKED BACK AND FORTH)

ROWS 1 & 4 *Knit 1, purl 1; repeat from* to end of row.

ROWS 2 & 3 *Purl 1, knit 1; repeat from * to end of row.

Repeat rows 1 through 4 for pattern.

BODY

With smaller needle, cast on 156 (174, 192, 210) stitches. Place marker to indicate beginning of round and join. Work in knit 1, purl 1 rib pattern until border measures 2½" (6.5cm). Work next round as follows: *knit 3, increase 1; repeat from * to end of round (increase by picking up yarn between stitches and knitting into the back of the loop creating a twisted stitch). You now have a total of 208 (232, 256, 280) stitches. Switch to larger needle and start pattern. Work in pattern until piece measures 12 (12½, 13, 14)" [30.5 (31.5, 33, 35.5) cm] from cast-on edge.

DIVIDE FOR ARMHOLES

Work 104 (116, 128, 140) stitches in pattern to middle of round. Place remaining stitches on spare needle for front.

SIZES

Adult small (medium, large, x-large).

Loose-fitting blouson-style sweater with cowl neck to fit sizes 36 (40, 44, 48)" [91.5 (101.5, 112, 122) cm]

YARN

Sport-weight yarn, 1,200 to 1,800 yards (1,097 to 1,646 m).

The sample is knit with Morehouse Merino 2-Ply in Lilac (6 to 9 skeins)

NEEDLES

Size 4 (3.5mm): 29" (73.5cm) circular, or longer; 16" (40.5cm) for sleeves and cowl neck; set of double-pointed needles, same size, for narrower part of sleeve. Or size to obtain gauge.

Size 3 (3.25mm): 24" or 29" (61 or 73.5cm) circular for ribbed border at waist; set of double-pointed needles for sleeve cuff [size 4 (3.5mm) could be used for this if worked more tightly than sleeve body)]; spare circular needles used as stitch holders.

OTHER MATERIALS

Stitch marker, tapestry needle.

GAUGE

21 stitches and 34 rows = 4 inches (10cm) in double seed stitch pattern.

BACK

Turn, and work back (on wrong side) to beginning of row. Continue working back and forth until piece measures 10 (11, 12, 13)" [25.5 (28, 30.5, 33)cm] from armhole division. Put stitches on spare holding needle.

A closer look at Debbie's Sweater—sans Debbie.

Debbie preparing for a special event at the shop's kitchen. The hooked rug in the background depicts Morehouse Farm.

FRONT

Slip front stitches from first spare needle to working needle. Work in pattern until front measures 7 (8, 9, 10)" [18 (20.5, 23, 25.5)cm] from armhole division.

NECK SHAPING

Work short rows for neck decreases as follows: work 43 (48, 53, 58) stitches in pattern, turn, and work back to beginning of row.
SHORT ROWS Work 41 (46, 51, 56) stitches in pattern, turn, and work back. Next, work 39 (44, 49, 54) stitches, turn, and work back.

Continue in this manner working 2 fewer stitches every right side row until 33 (36, 41, 46) stitches remain on the needle. Continue on remaining stitches and work in pattern until piece is same length as back. Repeat at other end on front piece for right front, working short rows on the wrong side rows.

Now bind off shoulders together using three-needle bind-off. Align front and back piece parallel to each other, wrong sides facing out, and bind off together (see Three-Needle Bind-Off on page 89). The remaining stitches are for the back neck.

COWL NECK

With 16" (40.5 cm) circular needle, starting at right shoulder, pick up stitches as follows: 1 stitch per 2 rows along vertical part of front neck (after short rows); 1 stitch per stitch along back neck and front neck, plus 1 additional stitch between short rows; 2 additional stitches at each shoulder. Work 7" (18cm), or desired height of collar, in knit 1 purl 1 rib. Bind off very loosely in rib.

SLEEVES

Using shorter circular needle, pick up stitches around armhole opening as follows: with right side facing out, starting at underarm location, pick up 1 stitch per 2 rows on sweater, 1 additional stitch at shoulder and 1 at underarm location. Place marker to indicate beginning of the round and join. Work in pattern. Decrease 2 stitches (knit the first 2 stitches together, purl the last 2 stitches together) every 8th round to desired sleeve length (or 15, 15½, 16, 17"), allowing for a 2½" (6.5 cm) cuff. Switch to double-pointed needles when sleeve becomes too narrow for 16" (40.5 cm) circular needle. Work round before cuff as follows: *knit 1, knit 2 together; repeat from * to end of round. Switch to smaller double-pointed needles and work 2½" (6.5cm) in knit 1, purl 1 rib. Bind off loosely in rib. Repeat for other sleeve.

FINISHING

Weave in yarn tails.

YARN WEIGHT INDEX

INDEX

RESOURCES

Morehouse Farm Merino yarn is available at Sheep's Clothing, the farm's store located at 2 Rock City Road, Milan, New York 12571 (telephone: 845-758-2816), or at the farm's online store, www.morehousefarm.com.

The yarn is also available at select yarn shops throughout the country. For a complete list of stores, contact www.morehouseyarn.com or call 845-758-6493

ABOUT THE CONTRIBUTORS

Albrecht Pichler and Margrit Lohrer

MARGRIT LOHRER grew up in Switzerland. Her mother taught her to knit when she was about four years old.

As a teenager she knit baby outfits and blankets for refugees from the Hungarian Revolution, and plenty of cool-looking (by 1950's standards) boatneck sweaters for her boyfriends. Then she put her knitting aside for the next twenty years and worked as a graphic designer in New York City.

In 1977 she and her husband, Albrecht Pichler, bought a farm in Dutchess County and began raising Merino sheep. Ever since, her life has been BS (before sheep) or AS (after sheep).

ALBRECHT PICHLER is a part-time sheep farmer and a full-time architect.

CLARA AICH's approach to photography is as diverse as her projects. She has worked for cosmetic companies, publishing houses, and advertising agencies, and pursued her own artistic interests photographing flamenco dancers, graffiti art, and historic Hungarian cemetery sculptures. Animals are among her favorite subjects.

Clara Aich

ABOUT THE FARM

MOREHOUSE FARM has been featured in numerous publications, including the *New York Times*, *Martha Stewart Living* and *Forbes Magazine*; the farm and its sheep and shepherds have been shown on many TV stations, including ABC, CBS, and MTV.